101 Questions & Answers on
Women in the
New Testament

101 Questions & Answers on Women in the New Testament

Judith Schubert, RSM

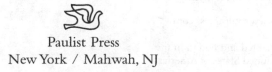

Paulist Press
New York / Mahwah, NJ

Cover image by Nicolo Orsi Battaglini / Art Resource, NY
Cover and book design by Sharyn Banks

Library of Congress Cataloging-in-Publication Data

Schubert, Judith, author.
    101 questions and answers on women in the New Testament / Judith Schubert, RSM, PhD.
        pages cm
    Includes bibliographical references.
    ISBN 978-0-8091-4845-5 (alk. paper) — ISBN 978-1-58768-294-0 (e-book)
    1. Women in the Bible—Miscellanea. 2. Bible. New Testament—Miscellanea. I. Title. II. Title: One hundred and one questions and answers on women in the New Testament. III. Title: One hundred one questions and answers on women in the New Testament.
    BS2445.S38 2014
    225.8`3054—dc23

                                                                    2013043244

ISBN 978-0-8091-4845-5 (paperback)
ISBN 978-1-58768-294-0 (e-book)

Published by Paulist Press
997 Macarthur Boulevard
Mahwah, New Jersey 07430

www.paulistpress.com

Printed and bound in the
United States of America

Contents

The 101 Questions and Answers

Chapter 1: General Questions

Chapter 4: The Gospel of Luke

Acknowledgments

I thank the Sisters of Mercy and Georgian Court University for their encouragement and support of a semester sabbatical to conclude research for this publication with Paulist Press. They provided me with the time to investigate, reflect, write, and edit the manuscript. I also thank family members, friends, colleagues, as well as students and attendees of lectures that I have given. They represent the ones who have provided me with questions that appear in this book about women in the New Testament. Special thanks to Andrea Rittenhouse and Winifred Klimek, alumnae of Georgian Court University who assisted voluntarily with research and editing of this project. Additional thanks to Mary Basso, a University librarian, whose knowledge helped in bibliographic questions, and Eugenia Kelly, who edited the final version. To them I am most grateful for their precious time, expertise, and support.

This work has been dedicated to the loving women who have touched my life so deeply: family members, Sisters of Mercy, friends, colleagues, and students. May God's gracious care permeate their lives in every way.

Introduction

In 1990 Raymond Brown, a famed Johannine scholar, published the initial book in the *101 Questions and Answers* series with Paulist Press. His book responds to general questions about the Bible that have been asked throughout his years of teaching and lecturing. Since that time several books in the series have been published to address various sections and/or subjects of the Bible. These volumes intend to answer some of the many questions proposed by readers of the sacred text.

A few years ago, Paulist Press invited me to write another manuscript in the series. The chosen topic addresses women in the New Testament. The questions within the book have been asked by graduate and undergraduate students as well as by audiences to whom I have lectured. Since the questions have been requested by others, the topics of discussion originate with others. Subsequently, not all women in the New Testament have been included because inquiries about them did not surface.

The topic of women in the New Testament surfaces as a very important one in twenty-first-century Christianity. Since the percentage of women in these churches remains very high, it becomes imperative that women of faith understand their biblical foremothers. Moreover, Christian men, especially those who serve in ministry, also need to understand both named and unnamed women in the sacred text in their roles as faithful followers of Jesus. In this way, Christians will increase their knowledge and hopefully, their appreciation of the importance of biblical women as role models for leadership.

On a personal note, the importance of women as creative leaders has impacted my own life from birth. Women family members have taught by their example. From great-grandmothers,

grandmothers, aunts, siblings, and especially my gracious loving mother, these family foremothers have provided my life with the qualities of deep faith, compassionate leadership, and a hope in all people regardless of gender, skin tone, cultural background, or religious affiliation. Being immersed in such inclusive lived values, I encountered another set of women with a similar vision, namely, the Sisters of Mercy, a group with whom I became a grateful member. In the nineteenth century, Catherine McAuley from Dublin, Ireland, founder of the Sisters of Mercy, demonstrated a special regard for women and girls suffering from poverty and lack of education in the Irish cities and towns. Her kind leadership, deep wisdom, and compassionate ways continue to impact all her sisters, Mercy Associates, Mercy Core Groups, and Mercy Collegiate Societies throughout the world.

The brave and humble women leaders mentioned above received strength from the women who appear in the New Testament. As models of faithful discipleship, these biblical women inspired not only their fellow community members, but also Christians throughout the centuries. Some of the named women, such as Mary of Magdala, have had their reputations and lives maligned by others over the ages as a result of misreading New Testament texts. In this twenty-first-century moment, the time has come to acknowledge such mistakes and correct a misreading of the past so that these valiant women receive their rightful place in the history of Christianity.

Abbreviations and Terms

BCE	Before the Common Era (previously, "before Christ" [BC]).
CE	Common Era (previously, *anno domini*, in the year of our Lord [AD]).
Cycles A, B, C	The three-year cycle of liturgical readings for Sundays.
Deutero-Isaiah	The latter part of the prophetic Book of Isaiah in the Hebrew Bible (chapters 40 and following).
Deutero-Pauline	Letters in the New Testament written after the death of Paul of Tarsus.
Hebrew Bible	Old Testament.
Household Code	Codes in New Testament letters written after Paul that pertain to the behavior in family and/or Church households.
Household Churches	Private homes in which liturgies were celebrated, the earliest form of communal worship for Christians.
Judahites	The members of the tribes of Judah and Benjamin who lived in the Kingdom of Judah.
Luke-Acts	The two-volume work in the New Testament written by the same author.
NAB	New American Bible.

NIV	New International Version Bible.
NKJV	New King James Bible.
NRSV	New Revised Standard Version of the Bible.
NT	New Testament.
Torah	First five books of the Bible (Genesis, Exodus, Leviticus, Numbers, and Deuteronomy).
WBC	*Women's Bible Commentary.*

Chapter 1

General Questions

1. What was the place of Jewish women in Greco-Roman society during the time of Jesus?

The lives of first-century CE Jewish women in Palestine were marked by a religious observance to the laws of Torah and other sacred books, the sayings of renowned rabbis, and the cultural customs of Palestine. A daughter was a constant source of worry for the father because, from the moment of her birth, he had the obligation to protect her virginity. In the book of *Ben Sira* (*Ecclesiasticus*), an earlier work whose directives would have been heard in the first century CE, the author asks in 7:24, "Do you have daughters? Be concerned for their chastity....." Later, in 42:9–11, the author presents a long list of strict rulings for any daughter and comments that "a daughter is a secret anxiety to her father, and worry over her robs him of sleep." The first-century world valued the sexual purity of a girl until she married. Therefore, unlike their male siblings, some writings suggested that girls became quite limited in their geographical movement in order to protect them from the desires of men. Unlike their brothers, girls should not venture out into public and should be confined to the private sphere of the home. Once a woman married, she went from the protection of her father to that of her husband. While the rabbis promoted marriage at an early age, the husband still became responsible for the sexual purity of his wife.

According to authors like Ben Sira, a woman's gender made her unequal to any male. In 42:14, he says: "Better is the wickedness of a man than a woman who does well; it is woman who

1

brings shame and disgrace." In varied rabbinic sources, the differing laws for men and women were justified with descriptions about the light-mindedness, gluttony, jealousy, or the strong odor of women. The famous Jewish historian, Josephus, mimics these beliefs when he proclaims in his last work, *Contra Apion* (2. 201), that "in every respect women are inferior to men." According to certain primary writings, therefore, women count for little in the world of the ancients.

For the past two decades, some biblical scholars have used such rabbinical and other historical works to describe the plight of Jewish women in the first-century world of Palestine. In recent times, however, authors such as Ross Kraemer (*Women & Christian Origins*) and Kathleen Corley (*Women and the Historical Jesus*) have written against viewing these primary sources as reliable historical facts. Their writings question and even object to conclusions that have been reached from a misreading of rabbinical and other ancient Jewish sources, such as the writings of Ben Sira, Philo of Alexandria, and Josephus.

I do agree with many of their points. For example, the lives of Jewish women of Palestine probably did not differ much from the lives of other women in the Greco-Roman world in that time. Of course, any free movement depended on the individual economic status of the families into which they were born. While I hold that women's participation in life outside the home remained curtailed, they still participated in public worship and the economic life of the village or city in some ways. I agree with Kraemer and Corley that women probably had more contact with others depending on their geographical and economic circumstances.

Jesus lived in Palestine during the first half of the first century CE. Like his fellow Jews, he lived under Roman occupation his entire lifetime. As such, he would have been greatly influenced by Hellenistic culture. (Hellenism represents a combination of Hellenic and Roman cultures). Therefore, the women who followed him lived under the same influence permeating Hellenistic culture in Palestine. Depending on economic status, their Gentile equivalents would sometimes be literate, educated in certain areas, hold positions of authority in both religious and societal areas, as well as run businesses. So, too, some Jewish women would have possessed similar strengths and accomplishments.

2. Why are women mentioned so rarely in the New Testament? Was that usual for the first century?

As a preliminary, we must remember that in general, the Bible was authored by men for the purpose of educating other men. Therefore, you may notice gender bias within the sacred text.

The New Testament writings reflect some of these cultural practices found in the Hebrew Bible. For example, in the first three Gospels of Mark, Matthew, and Luke, women often come into the text briefly and quickly leave like some of their male counterparts. Frequently, they do not appear as an integral part of the story. We must keep in mind, however, that these nameless and speechless women may have been more involved in the story than the text allows. The women who followed Jesus, and those of the early Christian communities, probably participated much more in the Jesus movement than appears in the text. Fortunately, some of the NT writings do demonstrate the presence of women leadership despite their absence in many texts.

For example, in John 4, the unnamed Samaritan woman takes on a leadership role in her own village after her encounter with Jesus. In John 11, at the time of the mourning of the death of her brother Lazarus, Martha of Bethany dialogues with Jesus in words that represent leadership. In John 21, Jesus chooses only Mary of Magdala to spread the glorious news of his resurrection to the other apostles.

Furthermore, earlier authentic Pauline writings acknowledge women as leaders in the Christian communities of Paul (e.g., Rom 16; Phil 4:2–3; Gal 3:28). So, too, Luke's Acts of the Apostles cite instances of women missionaries and leaders such as Tabitha (Acts 9:36), Lydia (Acts 16:14–15), and Prisca (Acts 18:2–3).

3. Can you give an example of how Jewish women of the New Testament could have been influenced by the women of the Hebrew Bible/Old Testament?

Jewish women, who appear in the New Testament, would have heard stories about women from the Book of Genesis, such as Eve, Sarah, Rebekah, Rachel, and so on. They would have heard about Jochebed, the mother of Miriam and Moses, and the midwives, Shiphrah and Puah from the Book of Exodus. Moreover, other heroines, such as, Ruth the Moabite, Judith, as well as Deborah the prophet/judge, probably would have been known by them through stories both from the Bible as well as from extended biblical stories (*midrashim*) of the rabbis.

One of the clearest examples of women from the Hebrew Bible influencing women in the New Testament appears in the Gospel of Luke. When the pregnant Mary visits her cousin Elizabeth and proclaims the beautiful canticle of thanksgiving, "My soul magnifies the Lord…" in Luke 1:47–55, the Lukan author has her echo the prayer of Samuel's mother, Hannah in 1 Samuel 2:1–10. Another example in Luke is in the next chapter (Luke 2:36–38), when Anna the prophet meets Mary and Joseph in the Jerusalem temple. As prophet, Anna represents the mouthpiece of God, one who speaks for the Divine. Moreover, as a widow she worshipped and fasted daily in the temple. Consequently, her praise of the child Jesus as redeemer would have been taken seriously. This New Testament figure joins other famous women prophets in the Hebrew Bible such as Miriam, Deborah, and Huldah.

Miriam, the sister of Moses and Aaron and identified as a prophet in Exodus 15:20, leads the people in a victory song and dance as they escape safely to freedom from the slavery of the Egyptians. So, too, in Luke 2:38 Anna the prophet leads the temple bystanders in hope as she proclaims the importance of the child, Jesus, to all in Jerusalem who awaited the redemption of Israel. Deborah, identified as both prophet and judge in Deuteronomy 4:4, gave confidence to her people through her continued guidance as well as her leadership role in the defeat of the oppressive Canaanite enemy. While Anna the prophet plays no role in directing battles, she does bring a hope of future salvation through her joyous praise to God for the child Jesus in their midst. Finally, Huldah, a prophet in the time of King Josiah, appears in both 2 Kings 22:14 and 2 Chronicles 34:22. In both instances, she advises this King of Judah in her role as God's prophet. So, too, does Anna in Luke 2, where she offers her fellow Jewish worshippers in the Jerusalem temple a promise of salvation through the child, Jesus. We will discuss these prophetic figures further in the answer to Question 31.

4. Why are none of the New Testament books written by women?

First, remember that we do not know the authorship of most books in the Bible. The collection stems from anonymous authorship. Scholars still hold that generally the books of the New Testament had male authorship, although periodically one suggests that a book or sections of a book may have been authored by a woman. However, support for such theories has not been strong because most women never had an opportunity for formal education. Their illiteracy would prohibit reading or writing a text.

Even though women of the Greco-Roman society made progress in some participation in the public sphere, rather than just the private space of their homes, life still functioned amidst a male-dominated social order. Consequently, society would most likely accept the writings of men, especially when it came to sacred texts. Later in subsequent centuries, we do encounter some later NT apocryphal writings about women such as the *Acts of Thecla* or *The Gospel of Mary of Magdala*. While these women figures emerge as heroines in the narrative, they do not appear to author the works themselves.

Also, remember that all books, which became part of the canon centuries later, had to be accepted by male leaders of the Church. This process took hundreds of years of development, amidst discussion, debates, additions, and elimination of books that reflected rising heresies both within and outside the Church. On this point, I suggest these decision makers accepted a particular book chiefly because of its frequent liturgical inclusion in various Christian communities. The decisions of the leaders reflect the attitudes of their times. Overall, neither canonical nor later patristic Christian sources exhibit the important role of women in early Christianity, partly because such writings were aimed at a literate male audience of Church leaders.

5. Does Jesus ever state in the New Testament that women are unfairly treated and men should treat them as equals?

No. In the Gospels, Jesus never addresses the issue. From even a cursory reading of the Gospels it remains clear that Jesus had a deep concern for the poor, the marginalized, and the outcasts of society. Naturally, many people of these three categories included women. While he did not address the status of women directly, his miracles, parables, and discourses encompassed a deep concern both for them as well as their situations.

As a Jew of Palestine, Jesus remained faithful to the laws of Torah. At the same time, however, occasionally he presented a more expansive interpretation of them. According to the Gospels, Jesus offered all people, not just his fellow Jews, access to God through his teachings and actions. Here women would benefit from his open invitations to God because Jesus never treats women different from men. Jesus demonstrates that he offers women full humanity and equality, through his words, attitude, and actions toward them. In particular, the reality of women disciples, who traveled with Jesus and had been treated as equals to their male counterparts, established equality between the two genders. Therefore, Jesus accepted women being outside the confines of their homes.

Furthermore, women did more than travel with Jesus as disciples. We learn from the Martha and Mary story in Luke 10:38–42 that he welcomed them to learn from him in his role as teacher (rabbi) as well. In the ancient societies a master taught his disciples, who followed him. In the same way, Jesus taught women as well as men. In doing so, he encouraged their intellectual and spiritual pursuits. In effect, Jesus' inclusive treatment of women promoted a "discipleship of equals" (Elisabeth Schüssler Fiorenza, *In Memory of Her,* 154) among his followers. In other words, the texts of the Gospels offer no examples of Jesus treating women disciples any different from men because of gender.

6. Why do women in the New Testament seem to be peripheral to the story? Why are they often nameless?

Until more current contributions in textual analysis, scholars often held that women characters had only minor roles to play in the Gospel accounts. In addition to traditional portrayals of women as insignificant, the fact that many of these women remained nameless brought further cause to perceive them as peripheral. When they appeared nameless, their function seemed to diminish. For instance, the healing of Peter's mother-in-law (Mark 1:29–31; Matt 8:14–15; Luke 4:38–39), the women with a hemorrhage (Mark 5:25–34; Matt 9:20–22; Luke 8:43–48), and the woman who anointed Jesus' feet (Luke 7:36–50) provide a few examples of nameless women who ministered to or encountered Jesus. Yet, until more recent times, writers gave such women little notice. Their namelessness often left them forgotten by readers of the biblical text. Furthermore, without names, these women lacked individual identity and empowerment.

Now, however, with the onset of a broader textual analysis by serious biblical scholars, the women in these narratives have become much more central to research. In stories such as the nameless woman who anointed Jesus in Mark 14:3–9, Jesus' remark that "wherever the good news is proclaimed in the whole world, what she has done will be told in remembrance of her," takes on new meaning. Finally, we must still remember that the Gospel stories, which incorporate women into the text, serve as "paradigmatic remembrances, not comprehensive accounts" of encounters with Jesus, a phrase coined by Elisabeth Schüssler Fiorenza (*In Memory of Her*, 102). Since men most likely provided authorship of the Gospels and they wrote for other literate men, the presence of women in a story would not have arisen as a major concern. The Gospels intended primarily to focus on Jesus and his words, deeds, and person. For such reasons, women played a much larger role in life than the biblical narratives demonstrate.

7. If Jesus intended to include women in the early Church, why weren't his intentions carried forward into modern times? Why has the role of women in relation to the hierarchical structure of the Roman Catholic Church remained static?

During the lifetime of Jesus, no "early Church" existed. Remember that Jesus lived and died as a faithful Jew. We glean from the Gospels that certain men and women either had been called or chose to follow Jesus throughout his ministry. In its inception, this "Jesus movement" included mostly fellow Jews like Jesus. After his death, resurrection, and ascension, more people became initiated through baptism into this movement to follow Jesus, including both Jews and Gentiles. Eventually, about twenty years or so after the fall of the second temple and city of Jerusalem, Jewish Christians had to sever relations with Judaism because of tighter restrictions from within Judaism. Consequently, the early Christian community, which you identify as "Church," became independent of Judaism.

From the Gospels, we learn that Jesus did not necessarily have any revolutionary intention about women or other topics. He never addressed directly the question of gender. However, by both his words and actions he kept very open-minded about changes for women in the Greco-Roman society of Palestine and their advancing habits of movement, literacy, education, and leadership. As such, his decisions and optional conclusions about women often transcended the general mores or even religious legislation of that time period. He accepted women as disciples, which included traveling with him from place to place. These attitudinal allowances demonstrate complete openness about the status of women. Yet, no evidence exists to consider Jesus as a revolutionary for the direct cause of women.

The second part of this question goes beyond the scope of this book, so that I can only offer a brief summarized explanation. Simply put, the role of women in relation to the hierarchical structure of the Roman Catholic Church has *not* remained static. According to the authentic letters of Paul and years later, the Lukan Acts of the Apostles, women functioned as leaders in some of the earliest Christian communities. In these biblical texts, we learn that Paul of Tarsus worked along with women to lead local various communities of Christians, some of whom he established. Both Paul's letters and Acts mention women like Phoebe of Cenchrae (one of the two ports of the city of Corinth), Lydia of Thyatira, and Priscilla (Prisca) of Rome as workers and leaders along with Paul in the ministry of the Gospel.

However, years later, Christian communities took on a new structural form, identified by Elisabeth Schussler Fiorenza as the "patriarchalization of the early Christian movement and ascendancy of the monarchical episcopacy" (*In Memory of Her*, 309–10). In such structures, the leadership roles of women diminished because of segregation and restrictions imposed on women. Perhaps the two opposing messages, one of a theology of equals as a result of baptism and the other, one of a societal degradation of women, caused a break in equality between the genders. Throughout the centuries and to this present day the Church has struggled with differing theological arguments regarding the equality of all the baptized in Christ.

8. Did women in early Christianity have any leadership roles within the community?

Yes, women in early Christianity did indeed lead Christian communities throughout the Greco-Roman world. When we open the pages of the New Testament, particularly in the Gospels, we read about special women who followed and lived as disciples of Jesus. As faithful role models to others, these women lead exemplary lives of compassionate service and openness to whatever would affect them in their futures.

In the early shaping of Christianity, names of various women leaders emerge both in the authentic letters of Paul and Acts of the Apostles. According to various New Testament texts, women functioned in roles such as "apostles" (Rom 16:7), "deacons" (Rom 16:1), heads of household Churches (Rom 16:5), theological teachers (Acts 18:26), and prophets (1 Cor 11:5).

In addition to passages from the New Testament about women leaders, other textual evidence appears in non-canonical literature that depicts the leadership of Mary of Magdala, such as *The Gospel of Mary*, a late second-century gospel or early third-century writing. While only fragments of this work remain, they, nevertheless, represent the only known gospel dedicated to a woman. The texts in these fragments reflect the authority of Mary the apostle as a source for the male apostles.

Besides literary textual evidence, other historical sources such as epigraphic texts inform us of the practices of women as ecclesiastical leaders in the early centuries of Christianity. Epigraphs represent inscriptions placed on statues, tombs, walls, or books to describe a person or theme. Inscriptions of women as apostles, prophets, presbyters, teachers, deacons, stewards, and even bishops appear in various texts, on tombstones, monuments, and in other ancient texts. In her book, *Women Officeholders in Early Christianity*, Ute Elsen demonstrates clearly and carefully that Christian women held active official leadership positions within the Church. In these cases, they would have been given specific titles. In addition, other women functioned in leadership roles without an official title from the community. In both categories, women emerge as dynamic makers of ecclesiastical history during the early centuries of the Church.

9. Why is Mary, mother of Jesus, so revered and yet mentioned so infrequently in the Gospels?

When we realize that the authors of the Gospels centered their attention on the revelation of the good news about Jesus, the Christ, we come to understand why other important figures were seldom addressed for any length of text. As a literary form, a Gospel presents the good news about Jesus as the Christ to others. As such, the four canonical versions of the Gospel do not concentrate on any other persons such as the important figure of Mary, his mother.

As we search the biblical texts, very few narratives pertain to Mary. In the earliest reference to Mary, she is even unnamed. In the Letter to the Galatians, Paul of Tarsus states that "God sent his son *born of a woman*" (Gal 4:4). Years later the Gospel of Mark contains two references to Mary (Mark 3:32, 34–35 and 6:3), which by the way, do not focus on the person of Mary, but as we may suspect, on the person of Jesus, the Christ. Moreover, the references to Mary in the Gospel of Mark do not compliment Mary.

The Gospel of Luke offers a powerful portrait of Mary in the opening chapters of the Gospel, called the "infancy narrative." In contrast to Mark, the Lukan author presents much softer statements about Mary and even presents dialogue from her. Luke uses his infancy narrative to highlight Mary's voice in three scenes: the announcement by the Angel Gabriel and the conversation with Mary (Luke 1:26–38), the visit between Elizabeth and Mary (1:39–58), and the finding of her lost twelve-year old son, Jesus, in the

Jerusalem temple (2:41–51). In all three scenes, the texts honor Mary as faithful "mother" and "disciple" in her covenant with God.

Luke's final mention of Mary occurs at the beginning of his second volume, namely, the Acts of the Apostles. Acts 1:14 states, "All these were constantly devoting themselves to prayer, together with certain women, *including Mary the mother of Jesus….*" In contrast to her other appearances in the infancy narrative, where Mary speaks, in this story she remains passive. Even in this brief and final portrayal of Mary, Luke portrays Mary as a model of "motherhood" and "faithful disciple."

Unlike Luke, the Gospel of Matthew communicates the announcement about Jesus' birth and the birth itself from the viewpoint of Joseph. Nevertheless, in his opening genealogy of Jesus, the evangelist includes four women from the Hebrew Bible, whose names appear before the insertion of Mary's name. Beverly Roberts Gaventa (*Mary: Glimpses of the Mother of Jesus*, 38) reminds us that all of these women experienced "both extraordinary or irregular sexual unions which appeared to be scandalous and… they took some initiative in their situations and were part of God's plan for the coming of the Messiah." Matthew brought these women into the genealogy to pre-figure Mary, whose pregnancy undoubtedly became suspect since she had not yet married Joseph.

All five women in the genealogy had circumstances in their lives that did not fit the ordinary behavior of women, but testified to the unpredictable and surprising ways of God. The interruption of the male list by the addition of the women provides strength to the inclusion of Mary in 1:16, who concludes the genealogy. When the evangelist inserts the name of Mary, he clearly wants to address possible attacks against Mary. Consequently, in 1:16, she receives the honorable title as the mother of Jesus the Messiah. In addition, her marriage can no longer be suspect because Joseph is named as her husband.

Yet, here in Matthew's infancy narrative the roles of men are heightened, while the role of Mary remains limited. She remains voiceless and sometimes even nameless (Matt 1:25).

The Gospel of John parallels the other Gospels in its rare mention of Mary. As a matter of fact, the author never even uses the name, "Mary," to refer to her. Rather, he uses the title "mother," a reminder that Jesus is both human and divine. Two times Mary appears within the Johannine text: the wedding feast of Cana, John 2:1–11 and the crucifixion scene, John 19:25–26. In both instances, the adult Jesus speaks to his mother. In this way, the stories in the fourth Gospel go beyond the announcement and birth narratives in Matthew and Luke, because the evangelist reveals a deepening relationship between Mary as mother and Jesus as son.

These two instances mark the only times that Mary surfaces in the fourth Gospel. In both stories, Jesus calls his mother, "woman." While this address may seem offensive for us in the twenty-first century, in ancient times "woman" (*gunai*) served as a title of respect. As the "mother" of Jesus helped to usher in the messianic times in the Cana narrative, so too, she plays a significant part at the foot of the cross by giving birth symbolically to a Christian community.

10. What's the *Gospel of Mary*? Which Mary?

While discussion still occurs about verification of the proper name in the title, I advocate that the *Gospel of Mary* refers to Mary of Magdala. To date, it remains the only gospel named after a woman. Until recently, the *Gospel of Mary* has mainly been considered a Gnostic text, but today not all scholars agree. Gnosticism derives from the Greek word, *gnosis*, meaning "knowledge." As a philosophical movement, it envisioned the human soul being trapped in a material world by an *inferior* divine being. Gnosticism refers to the revealed knowledge that some humans receive to bring them back to the *superior* Godhead.

In spite of the ongoing discussion about its origin, scholars need to look at the work in a broader context, that is, one that provides a real glimpse of the types of questions, discussion, and practices in the early centuries of Christianity. For example, the manuscript gives important credibility to the leadership of women, it provides a source for the role of women in the Christian communities, and it highlights the role of spirituality. It also exposes resentment toward women in their roles as teachers, credible witnesses, and recipients of Jesus' revelations to them. Finally, it downplays the erroneous view of modern Christians about an idyllic life within the early Church.

Despite the absence of large portions of the text, the *Gospel of Mary* credits Mary of Magdala as a leader of and teacher to the disciples. Unlike the other Gospels that include narratives about Jesus during his lifetime as well as after his resurrection, this gospel centers on visions and revelations to Mary from Jesus after his departure from earth. An overall summary of the text includes the following points: After the departure of Jesus, the disciples worry and become somewhat fainthearted about their mission to go and preach to others. At this moment, Mary comforts and encourages them to be strong as she reminds her fellow disciples of the greatness of the Savior (Jesus).

Even though the *Gospel of Mary* does not appear as one of the four Gospels within the New Testament canon, it can be an important teaching tool for us in the twenty-first century. The document encourages us to open our hearts and minds to the workings of God. Gender bias does not reflect God's intention as proclaimed in the opening chapter of the entire Bible, where God created man and woman as equals (Gen 1:27).

11. In the birth stories about Jesus in the Gospels of Matthew and Luke, why doesn't Mary suffer any labor pains?

When we read the infancy narratives (birth stories) in both the Gospels of Matthew and Luke, we realize that many points about Mary have not been included. For example, did her parents help her? Did she have a midwife? This leads to your question about birth pains. The infancy narratives neither support nor oppose the idea of Mary having birth pains; instead, they ignore the subject. Remember that, in general, the purpose of the Gospels would have been to focus on Jesus. In particular, the infancy narratives were written to defend Jesus as the true Messiah. Therefore, Mary's birth pains would not be significant to the writers.

A few centuries after the writing of the Gospels, the portrayal of Mary evolved, especially in the Western Church, from Mary as "mother" to Mary as "ever virgin." At that time, many ecclesiastical leaders held up Mary as the obedient model of contemplative discipleship, to be admired for her belief and obedience to God, rather than for biological motherhood. Mary, ever virgin, would be used as a model for all, especially women. This disassociation from female sexuality lessened the dignity of women as "mothers" because of the emphasis on Mary as "virgin." No married women could ever live up to this image of Mary as role model.

Chapter 2

The Gospel of Mark

12. In Mark 1:30, Simon/Peter has a mother-in-law, so he must have been married. Why don't we hear about his wife? What about the other disciples' wives?

The miracle story in Mark 1:29–31 definitely leads readers to conclude that Peter has a wife. However, in the brief narrative, only a nameless mother-in-law has been mentioned. After she has been cured by the gentle hand of Jesus, the mother-in-law arises from her bed and begins serve them. In doing so, she acts as one in charge, that is, as a gracious hostess of the house, perhaps because she owned it. This house probably served as a headquarters for Jesus' ministry after he left Nazareth. It may have even served as his "second home" (Matt 4:13).

In 1 Corinthians 9:5, Paul poses a rhetorical question: "Do we not have the right to be accompanied by a believing wife, as do the other apostles and the brothers of the Lord and Cephas [Peter]?" Paul's remarks make it clear that the apostles, including Peter, have wives. While Peter's wife has no identification or name in this passage, later tradition in the early Church suggests that she ministered along with Peter. Clement of Alexandria, a late second-century theologian/philosopher related that Peter's wife died a martyr. Clement declares: "It is said that blessed Peter, seeing his wife led to death, felt joy because of her call and her return home and that he encouraged her and consoled her, calling her name and saying: 'Remember the Lord!'" (*Stromata* VII:11).

17

In Mark 1:29–30, then, Peter's mother-in-law embodies the role of a woman in a male-dominated society, that is, to provide for the domestic needs of all in the house. As expected, she also remains in closed quarters to preserve modesty and avoid encountering men. Despite such cultural limitations, this woman, only known as Peter's mother-in-law, becomes a true model of service for others in Christianity.

13. In Mark 3:31–35, are Jesus' sisters and brothers actual siblings?

Mark 3:31–35 is one of the many passages in the New Testament that allude to the brothers/sisters of Jesus. Other texts include: Mark 6:3; Matthew 1:24–25, 12:46; John 2:12; 7:3–5; Acts 1:14; and Galatians 1:19.

An answer to the affiliation between Jesus and "brothers and sisters" seems more crucial when, in many New Testament texts, James, the brother of Jesus, arises as the leader of the Church in Jerusalem (Gal 1:19–20; 2:9, 12; 1 Cor 15:7; Acts 12:17; 15:13; 21:18). John Donahue and Daniel Harrington (*The Gospel of Mark*, 187–8) summarize the three foremost historical responses to the debate over this question throughout the centuries:

1. First, the ancient Church held that the brothers and sisters of Jesus did indeed have Mary and Joseph as their parents. These children would have been born after Jesus (Matt 1:25). This tradition appears in the works of Hegesippus (second century CE), Tertullian (160–220 CE), and Helvidius (fourth century CE), whose work has not been discovered, but whose comments have been encased in the rebuttals of Jerome.

2. Second, the Epiphanian solution (fourth century), probably stems from a second-century work, entitled *The Infancy Gospel of James*. This non-canonical gospel text states that Joseph, a widower, had been chosen to marry the twelve-year-old Mary by the priests of the Jerusalem temple after

they witnessed a divine sign. ("Infancy Gospel of James" in *The Complete Gospels*, 387).

3. Third, the hypothesis from Jerome, who claimed that the "brothers and sisters" of Jesus mentioned in the biblical texts, indicate the "cousins" of Jesus.

The three major opinions exemplify the differing views among both scholars and Christians. In modern times, both Roman Catholic and other Christian scholars, especially in the Lutheran-Catholic dialogue have worked together to come to a greater unity regarding differences of thought in biblical texts, dogma, sacraments, and other historical and theological traditions. As a result, many biblical scholars hold that the New Testament does not address the continued virginity of Mary, a point that affects the question about the "brothers and sisters" of Jesus. The results of such serious study produce a variety of interpretations that do not dishonor the biblical text. With all this in mind, the dogma of the Roman Catholic Church today continues to follow the thought of Jerome, namely, that Mary remained a virgin. In this framework, the "brothers and sisters" of Jesus refer to cousins.

14. In Mark 5:25–34, what is the significance of the woman hemorrhaging for twelve years? Wouldn't she be dead from blood loss by then?

In Mark 5:25, the translated phrase "suffering from hemorrhages" comes from the Greek *rusei haimatos*, which means "a flow of blood." The exact Greek phrase appears in Leviticus 15:25 of the Septuagint (Greek translation of the Hebrew Bible) to describe prolonged occurrences of vaginal bleeding. Therefore, the phrase signifies a severe diminishment of the woman's quality of life in several ways. A ritually unclean woman would be banned from important activities in her life, such as joining family or village celebrations, going to synagogue or to the Jerusalem temple. In other words, the unclean woman must avoid any contact with others until she becomes ritually clean. In particular, she could not touch anyone because the other person would then become unclean. Besides the levitical regulations, the woman would have been under any additional rabbinic policies that had been established by the time of Jesus.

In 5:25, the evangelist relates that the woman has been in this state for twelve years. If the woman hemorrhaged continually, she would be dead long before this time. Since the author relates nothing of the intensity of the "flow of blood," it would be reasonable to conclude that the discharge may not have been continuous or always heavy because she remains alive and at least somewhat active after all these years. In any case, being cast as "unclean" for this length of time would truly weaken the woman physically, emotionally, and socially.

15. In Mark 5:27–28, what is the significance of the hemorrhaging woman touching Jesus? Usually he is the one who does the touching in the healing stories.

Your question about the significance of that touch has many replies. Three negative points result from the woman's decision. By going out into public, the unclean hemorrhaging woman has violated the Jewish religious purity code from Leviticus 15:25. Additionally, her touch violates such codes since any woman could make a man unclean by touching him during her monthly period. By handling his garment, this woman makes Jesus unclean.

More importantly, on the positive side, the suffering victim exhibits great faith in the powers of Jesus. She also demonstrates a consistent courage from the many doctors that she has visited to the brave decision to go out into public and touch the outer garment of Jesus. In 5:31, when Jesus realizes that power had gone out from him and asks, "Who touched my clothes?" the woman steps forward. The healed woman displays her strong character and deep integrity as she comes forward courageously to explain her actions and to accept whatever decision will be in store for her. Jesus' remarkable response ignores her breach of purity regulations and praises her strong inner spirit as he announces, "Daughter, your faith has made you well; go in peace and be healed of your disease" (5:34).

This dramatic threefold proclamation draws some remarkable conclusions. By calling her "daughter," Jesus adapts the conventional culture of fathers being in charge of their daughters and he, too, acts like a father who cares for his offspring. When he acknowledges, "your faith has made you well," Jesus credits the woman for her own cure because of her unwavering belief, inner strength, and bold actions. As he bids her, "go in peace," he uses a common Jewish greeting of "*shalom*," to offer the woman wholeness of life and blessings for it. His last comment, "be healed of your disease," exemplifies the results of the woman's open heart and stance of bravery. This courageous woman of gratitude becomes a model of trust, perseverance, and force for others who suffer from their own health-related issues. Lastly, she offers hope for women today to continue forging new cultural and social boundaries in the area of leadership, initiative, and religious law.

16. In Mark 7:25, why did the Syrophoenician woman bow down at Jesus' feet?

The account of the Syrophoenician woman in Mark 7:24–30 opens with Jesus traveling to a territory outside of Palestine, namely Phoenicia. As he journeyed he entered someone's home for privacy. A Gentile (non-Jewish) woman from that territory who had heard about him, sought him there. When she had found him at the house, she fell down at the feet of Jesus.

In response to the question as to the "why" of her subservient stance of bowing at the feet of Jesus, remember that such a posture demonstrates a person's awe and reverence for the one who receives the gesture. Throughout the ancient world, bowing would be a sign of deep respect, especially in reference to the Caesar/King. Since the woman would have been a citizen of the Phoenician republic of Tyre and governed by the province of Syria, she assuredly would be very different than Jesus in religion and culture. Therefore, her humble stance demonstrates her profound respect for the person of Jesus. Further, it also confirms her untold grief about the plight of her daughter. Like the woman with a hemorrhage, this woman remains unnamed, displays daring courage, and enters into a space without invitation because she seeks a greater good, the wellness of her child.

17. In Mark 7:26, how and why did a demon possess the woman's daughter?

Any answers to the questions of "how" and "why" the demon possessed the woman's daughter cannot be gleaned from the story itself. The author gives no indication of the reason for or the beginning of the illness. To help understand the ancient meaning of "being possessed," contemporary scholars make the following observations.

In the ancient Sumerian and Akkadian literature from Mesopotamia, the concept of demon possession refers to all people who had unusual human behavior, such as uncontrollable muscle movement, unrecognizable or slurred speech, as well as people with mental disorders. Actually, any unacceptable type of behavior received the unfortunate label of demon possession. Eventually, these cultures and religions personified the evil in the belief that some evil spirit penetrated the victim's body with the intent of causing evil or harm.

By the time of the New Testament, the topic of demons appears less frequently, and often only in connection with exorcisms. In some New Testament texts, such as those in Mark, the term for "demon" becomes interchangeable with the term "spirit." In these cases, a qualified adjective precedes "spirit," such as, the term "unclean spirit," which surfaces in this particular miracle story. In Mark 7:26, 29, then, the belief that the daughter had been possessed by some "unclean spirit/demon," derives from the influence of Mesopotamia and the oral traditions as well as written intertestamental texts that precede this writing.

18. In Mark 7:27, Jesus' words to the Gentile woman seem harsh. Why wouldn't Jesus wish to heal her daughter?

When the woman begged Jesus to heal her stricken daughter from a demon, Jesus curtly remarked in 7:27, "Let the children be fed first, for it is not fair to take the children's food and throw it to the dogs." Your comment, about the "harsh" words of Jesus and his disregard for her person or plea, addresses an impatience and disrespect for which any reader would be shocked to attribute to him. Therefore, let us look closely at two words, "children" and "dogs," in this particular verse.

In 7:27, the term *children* refers to the daughters and sons of Israel, namely, the Jews. Here Jesus the Jew proclaims the beliefs of Judaism. As the chosen ones of God, they act as the claimers of God's benefits. At the end of the sentence, Jesus protests against taking the children's food in order to "throw it to the dogs." The word *dog* has been used from ancient times as an insult, and still appears today in the form of a reference to a female dog. For the Jews, "dogs" have always been viewed in a negative light because they represent one of the categories of unclean animals. Consequently, when Jesus associated the term, "dogs" with the grieving mother, he verbalized a biting insult upon her. He insinuates that he rejects the Gentiles as recipients of his curative powers.

In viewing the entire scene, Jesus' initial rebuff of the woman may result from a variety of factors such as personal tiredness, his need for privacy, her ritual uncleanliness, or a view that this unknown woman overstepped her social and/or religious boundaries. In any case, the story does not end on this caustic note. Recall in 7:27 that Jesus also employs the qualifier, "first" in regard to the "children" (Jews), which seems to indicate that another feeding will take place. It seems plausible that the "second" feeding of divine aid would be given to non-Jews, namely, the Gentiles.

19. In Mark 7:28, the woman's response seems out of character for a female of the time. What is that all about?

Yes, in this scene, the woman does act out of character for a female of that time in many ways: her coming out to seek Jesus; her self-invitation into the place where he rested; her approach to an unknown man; and, her speaking in public at all. Her bravery in deed and speech exemplifies sheer determination to help her sick daughter. Deep love for a child motivates disrespectful action.

The woman, who had just received such a scathing response in the previous verse (7:27), replies in a non-offensive way. Even though she has just been called a "dog," the woman appears to take no offense. In doing so, she embraces the selfless role of a mother and strong believer in Jesus. The woman's mature attitude shines forth as she addresses Jesus as "Sir."

In a very clever fashion, the woman repeats the dishonorable slur of "dog" to receive the necessary help for her daughter: "Sir, even the *dogs* under the table eat the children's crumbs." This bold retort indicates that as a Gentile, she recognizes that she would be considered a "dog" by Jews. She also realizes from his remarks that Jesus calls the Jews "children," and that his concern remains for them first, rather than for those outside Judaism. However, despite unwelcoming remarks and attitudes, the woman did not turn away ashamed. Rather, she takes this moment of dishonor and turns it into a moment of opportunity. In 7:28, the woman answers Jesus in a courageous and humble manner by challenging him to become more inclusive. While initially Jesus did not seem to want to act on her behalf, he changes his mind after he hears her words of wisdom and witnesses her deep love for her daughter as well as her profound faith in him.

The controversy ends and the woman triumphs. Through her unwavering faith in Jesus, her humble persistence, and continued challenging wisdom, Jesus changes his mind and responds positively to her request. In essence, this miracle story provides an excellent example of how the unnamed woman, who seemed to have had no authority in ancient society, influenced a decision of Jesus, one that affected both their lives.

20. In Mark 14:3, who is this woman who anoints Jesus and why would she do so?

This dramatic account serves as an anointing of Jesus in preparation for his death and burial, and inaugurates the passion narrative, which details the events of Jesus' passion, death, and resurrection. Within the narrative, the generous actions of this unnamed woman reflect an ancient biblical ritual in the selection of a community leader. The anointing of a head with oil often by a prophet became a recognizable practice in the coronation ceremony of kings in the Hebrew Bible (e.g., 1 Sam 10:1, where Samuel as prophet/judge anoints Saul; 1 Kgs 1:34–40, where Nathan the prophet anoints Solomon).

The identity of the woman herself remains unknown in Mark. Interestingly, in the Gospel of John, which came into existence about twenty to thirty years later, the writer names the woman as Mary of Bethany. Whereas in Mark, the unnamed woman pours ointment on the head of Jesus, in the Johannine version, Mary anoints the feet of Jesus and wipes them with her hair.

Accounts of anointing Jesus occur also in the two other Gospels. In Matthew 26:6–13, the writer follows the Markan text very closely. Luke's story of an anointing (7:36–50) does not have to do with any preparation for the death and burial of Jesus. Instead, the story takes place within the early ministry of Jesus and centers on the forgiveness of sins and a grateful heart on the part of a woman, who had sinned.

The woman in Mark 14:3, although she remains unnamed in this Gospel, does exhibit deep respect and love for Jesus. Due only to her generous gift of expensive ointment and courageous actions, Jesus receives an anointment at the conclusion of his ministry. Like some biblical prophets who preceded her, the woman functions as a prophet, whose actions predict the death of Jesus the Messiah.

21. In Mark 14:3–9, Jesus states that the woman who anointed him would be remembered always. Why was her name not given so we could remember her? Do we do anything special in the Church to facilitate that remembrance?

As I have stated in previous answers, the absence of identifying the woman with a name becomes all too frequent in the New Testament. Various reasons may arise for the lack of the woman's identity, such as: her name did not appear in the source; it did not occur to the writer to name the woman because in the first century CE, most women did not have authority outside their own home; women would not be acceptable as witnesses to a person or event and, therefore, a name would be of no importance to the story.

In regard to your question about what Christian churches do to facilitate her remembrance, Mark 14:3–7 functions as the Gospel reading on Passion (Palm) Sunday once every three years during the B cycle of readings. The Orthodox tradition has always maintained the belief that the different women in these anointing stories remain separate individuals. However, since the late sixth century CE, the Western Church has been affected by the preaching and writings of Pope Gregory the Great (*Homiliarum in evangelia*, Homily 33), who followed another tradition of combining all these anointing stories from the Gospels into one story and one character. He preached that the woman who anointed Jesus, whether named or unnamed, referred to Mary of Magdala, a great sexual sinner. Yet, no Gospel describes her in this way. So, how do we regain recognition for this unnamed woman so admirably praised by Jesus here in Mark 14:3–9? Remember that while others became angered and resentful of the woman's extravagant devotion, Jesus did not. Instead, he silences their complaints and extols her kindness to him. Finally, Jesus himself identifies her actions as prophetic and proclaims one of the strongest compliments that he gives to anyone in the Gospels: "Truly, I tell you, wherever the good news is proclaimed in the whole world, what she has done will be told in remembrance of her." As such, this nameless prophetic woman remains an influential figure whose wholehearted example of selfless love needs to be followed.

22. In Mark 15:40–41, why, of all Jesus' numerous disciples, are only the women mentioned at the crucifixion? The only men mentioned are the soldiers.

Mark never mentions that the male disciples followed Jesus' journey to death or stayed to view his horrific crucifixion.

Contrary to the frightened behavior of the male disciples, the women disciples remained faithful. In 15:40, the evangelist carefully states that the women including Mary of Magdala, Mary the mother of James and Joses, as well as Salome, "looked on from a distance." The phrase "from a distance," indicates that women's presence at Roman executions, which would have been carried out in a public place, was unacceptable in these ancient cultures. Even though Jesus' women disciples broke such barriers, they would not be accepted at such a scene of Roman capital punishment. Furthermore, it would have been very wise for the women not to attract any attention to circumvent any social or political danger at this emotional time of crucifixion.

In 15:41a, which comes immediately after the naming of the three women, it reads: "These (the three women) used to follow him and to provide for him when he was in Galilee." In two short verses, the evangelist Mark attributes to these three women a description of a true disciple of Jesus. He identifies these very special women as followers, providers, and witnesses to Jesus. All such descriptions make these women disciples of Jesus.

Lastly, in the second half of the Markan verse (15:41b), the evangelist states, "there were many other women who had come up with him to Jerusalem." Therefore, a larger group of women who had become disciples of Jesus also remained faithful and followed him to the end of his journey. Despite the fear of arrests, intimidation, and other serious dangers for choosing to stay with Jesus even from a distance, these faithful women stand as true examples of courage, fidelity, leadership, and love. While little appears about them in the Markan texts, their strong faith cannot be denied.

Chapter 3

The Gospel of Matthew

23. The genealogy found in Matthew 1:2–16 includes women. Why does Matthew include them?

The listing of women's names in an ancient genealogy occurs as a rare phenomenon indeed. Nevertheless, Matthew lists four women from the Hebrew Bible and Mary, the mother of Jesus from the New Testament within his list of several male names. By including these women, Matthew reconfigures the customary list of *patrilineage* to describe the important ancestry of Jesus.

The four women from the Hebrew Bible clearly share common elements. First, the women come from or marry into different religious and cultural backgrounds than would fully incorporated Israelites. Second, each of the four women had a moment of scandal in their union with their partners. Third, in Matthew's list, the first four women are listed in the same literary pattern ("by Tamar," "by Rahab," "by Ruth," "by the wife of Uriah").

Mary, the mother of Jesus and the wife of Joseph, appears in Matthew 1:16 as the last figure among the five named women in Matthew's genealogical list. Although Mary's circumstance differs in many ways from the other mentioned women, they all possess familiar elements that have affected both the history of Israel and later Christianity. Mary, like these women, kept an open heart to the divine workings in her life.

Why does Matthew include them? As we read biblical texts about these strong women, it becomes evident that each encoun-

29

tered a startling or unjust event/situation that changed the course of her life. Often they were threatened by the cultural mores and laws of their times. Despite dangerous situations, their belief in God remained steadfast. Due to their effective courage and enduring patience, they changed the course of biblical history for God's people. Despite their cultural and religious powerlessness, all five women serve as living examples of God's Spirit at work within them because of their open hearts and noble gestures.

Matthew's list of five commendable women offers a paradigm of true heroism and valor in a patriarchal world because they accept the challenges to work toward good despite the prejudice against them. Their lives exemplify a divine righteousness, rather than the righteousness of society. Powerless, these women rose to become Spirit-filled leaders. Matthew's inclusion of these women into the genealogy clearly demonstrates that God's ways often do not reflect the thinking of the world or religious institutions.

24. In Matthew 14:3, why did John the Baptist condemn Herod when he married Herodias, the wife of his half-brother Philip?

The married Herod Antipas, who reigned over Galilee as tetrarch, fell in love with Herodias, the wife of his half-brother, while he stayed with them in Rome. As a result, Herod Antipas abandoned his wife to be with Herodias. This union destroyed two marriages and broke Jewish laws (Lev 18:16; 20:21) against taking a brother's wife. Therefore, John the Baptist condemned the actions of Herod Antipas.

The condemnation of the couple's actions brought fear, anger, and resentment toward John the Baptist by both Herodias and Herod. Eventually, these emotions resulted in his murder. The unbridled actions of Herodias and Herod Antipas demonstrate the pain that self-serving choices have on so many others. Selfishness and passion alone never equal real love.

25. In Matthew 28:1, why were Mary Magdalene and the other Mary going to look in the tomb where Jesus had been laid?

In Matthew's Gospel, Jesus was anointed in Bethany prior to his death by a generous and perceptive woman. As a result, Jesus proclaims, "In pouring this ointment on my body, she has done it to prepare it for burial" (Matt 26:12). Perhaps for Matthew, then, Mary of Magdala and the other Mary went to the tomb for other reasons. As two faithful Jews, their visit to the tomb would be in accord with an accepted practice of mourning. Since Matthew's original intended audience were Jewish Christians, no explanation of the women's visit to the tomb would be necessary because they followed Jewish practices. Mary of Magdala and the other Mary did what any authentic disciple would do, namely, follow Jesus to the end. Their actions bespeak honor, fearlessness, and deep love. They represent the true followers, who stood by Jesus during his life, death, and resurrection.

26. In Matthew 28, an angel tells the women to go and tell the disciples that Jesus is not dead. Obviously, the women were commissioned to relay an earth-shattering message. Why have they been silenced throughout Church history?

In all four Gospels, women or a woman receive this "earth-shattering" news before the others. Clearly, this point in all the Gospels demonstrates a divine trust in the commitment of the women to Jesus. These first witnesses to the resurrection of Jesus become the first proclaimers of the good news.

Why, then, "have women been silenced throughout Church history"? This is a fundamental and burning question for many in the twenty-first century, and has many answers. Remember that before the rise of first-world modernism, the subordination and mistreatment of women was practiced socially, economically, politically, and even theologically. Women were not empowered because that would have gone against human nature according to cultural mores. We can see some of the ramifications of a male-dominated society in the separate mindsets of women and men, as well as in their traditions, such as who may occupy public and private space.

Carolyn Osiek questions whether the stories of the women at the tomb had yet been transmitted to the public sphere of knowledge. If stories are not promulgated for all to hear, they will never be known in the oral tradition ("The Women at the Tomb" in *A Feminist Companion to Matthew*, 215). Elaine Wainwright suggests that Gospel stories about women leadership or commissioning have been read for centuries as individual momentary flashes within the text. On the contrary, male commissions have been read as ongoing discipleship that carries lasting authorized leadership (*Shall We Look for Another?*, 116). As Christianity moved from early house Churches to formal structures, more hierarchal structures came into place that threatened the leadership and ministry of women. Francine Cardman indicates that by the fourth century CE, the process of institutionalization was almost complete. Yet, women still participated in some ministry and leadership. As a result, the "bishops and councils continued to issue protest and formal prohibitions of women's ministries well into the sixth century and beyond" ("Women, Ministry and Church Order in Early Christianity," in *Women & Christian Origins*, 300). The more the Church immersed itself in Roman society, the more it took on male hierarchal structures.

This left all decision-making, education, and ministerial leadership to men. Consequently, for centuries, many of the biblical heroines had no voice. Sacred texts about them were ignored, and the early women who played an essential role in the movement to follow Jesus were unknown in the Christian world.

Chapter 4

The Gospel of Luke

27. In Luke 1:7, was it really possible for an older couple like Zechariah and Elizabeth to conceive a child? What was the average age of death back then?

The Lukan author never mentions the ages of Zechariah and Elizabeth. He simply states in 1:7 that they "had no children, because Elizabeth was barren, and both were getting on in years." In biblical texts, to describe a couple as aging and childless signifies the human impossibility of child bearing. In other words, only God could cause such a pregnancy to take place. As for the life expectancy of people in the first-century Greco-Roman world, it depended on status, economic circumstances, and the like. Yet, even with all these considerations, life expectancy would be very different in the first century CE than it is today. Some modern Roman historians suggest that the average mortality rate would have been less than half of today's expected life span. As for women, we must remember that many would have died young after giving birth.

Anyone familiar with the Hebrew Bible recognizes the allusion that the evangelist makes to barren foremothers of past ages, such as Sarah (Gen 16–21), Rebecca (Gen 25:21), Rachel (Gen 30:1), and Hannah (1 Sam 1–2). Luke compares Elizabeth to such major figures in order to give her grand stature. Unfortunately, in these ancient times, society denounced barren wives as the ones who brought dishonor to both the husband and the family. Both the Jewish and Greco-Roman cultures often blamed wives for lack of descendants and attributed it to wrongdoing in their lives or the lives of their family. Yet, instead of accusation, Luke calls Elizabeth "righteous" without any hesitation (1:6). She emerges among those favored by God. As you read Luke's description of Elizabeth, you will also notice that every positive comment he makes about Zechariah, he also does of her. In accord with the greatness of her foremothers, Elizabeth clearly ranks among those to emulate.

28. In Luke 1:32, if Mary knew she had a special child, announced as the "Son of the Most High," how could she not have known Jesus was destined for greater things?

In Luke 1:32, the angel Gabriel promises Mary that she has been favored by God and that the child to be born to her will not be illegitimate in God's eyes. On the contrary, he will be "called the Son of the Most High...." This identification designates holiness and association with the divine (Luke 1:35, 76). In effect, the son to be born will be God's favored one.

In 1:32, your question about the child being called "Son of the Most High," continues with the next part of the same verse, which reads "and the Lord will give him the throne of his ancestor David." This reference back to 2 Samuel 7:12–13 assures Mary that her son will follow in the Davidic line. Thus, the angel Gabriel's message includes both scriptural references back to the Hebrew Bible as well as nationalistic societal overtones.

Now, to your basic inquiry of "how *could she not have known* Jesus was destined for greater things?" Your "historical" question about Mary's knowledge of her future son calls for an historical answer, but one cannot be given. Here, the biblical text needs to be read within the literary genre of a "gospel" ("good news" that is, *euaggelion*) and not as a biography. When Luke wrote this Gospel at least a half century after the time of Jesus, he did not intend it as a factual biography according to twenty-first-century standards.

Rather, he wrote from the perspective of his own generation and theological questions from at least a half century after Jesus.

29. How could Mary be so open-minded about the conception of her son in Luke 1:38 when she says, "Here am I, the servant of the Lord; let it be with me according to your word." Wouldn't she have known she would be an outcast if it were apparent that Joseph wasn't the father of the child?

In this scene, Luke depicts Mary as a model of authentic discipleship. While her words certainly threaten her acceptance by and status of her future in Joseph's household, she accepts the divine will over her own upcoming circumstances. Luke describes Mary as "a virgin engaged to a man whose name was Joseph" (Luke 1:27), the first part of a two-step marriage process that included a formal exchange of promises before witnesses and a dowry, giving the intended bridegroom sexual as well as legal control over the intended bride. Thus, Mary's historical situation would have caused her much emotional pain and grief from both families because being pregnant before the completion of the marriage brought dishonor and shame. To envision Mary's extremely difficult reply to the angel Gabriel as a lovely, joyful moment in the annunciation scene would be to dishonor her complete sacrifice to God. Finally, Mary's positive response to the angel has also been seen by some scholars as Luke's reinforcement in his belittling of women and exemplifies his portrayal of many women in Luke-Acts as passive, obedient, and silent. Mary's final remarks to the angel Gabriel, "Behold, the slave (*doulos*) of the Lord" (Luke 1:38, my translation), only strengthens their observations. On the contrary, Mary's completely selfless "yes" to God reflects her deep commitment and faith in the Divine. To agree in spite of the expected negative response from family and others, Mary had to be a strong and deeply committed woman of God and a true model of discipleship for all of us.

30. In Luke 1:56, it says that Mary stayed with Elizabeth for about three months. Why didn't she stay until John was born?

Your question about why Mary did not wait until the birth of Elizabeth's baby, whom we later know as John, needs some explanation. Barbara Reid (*Choosing the Better Part?*, 77) suggests that Luke used Mary's sudden departure to continue the story with other characters. In the third Gospel, women often enter and exit a scene quickly. So, too, here Luke intends to use Mary's sudden exit from the scene as a literary device to continue the narrative with the other characters. Remember that this story is an infancy narrative, not an historical biography. An infancy narrative intends to proclaim the birth of an important person. It does not aim to present detailed historical facts. In this narrative, Luke clearly intends to picture a close bond between the two women. This point furthers his comparison between the two annunciations, one to Zechariah about the birth of John and one to Mary about the birth of Jesus, as well as the two birth stories of these babies. By these associations, Luke intends to give continual prominence to Jesus over John.

The account of Mary's arduous journey to be with Elizabeth for an extended stay during both their pregnancies is intended to cement the comparison between the separate stories of the births. As the figure of Jesus supersedes that of John, so, too, the importance of Mary rises above that of Elizabeth as seen in Luke 2.

31. In reference to Luke 2:36 and the prophet Anna, were women prophets in Israel?

In the Hebrew Bible, woman prophets do emerge in and out of stories. In particular, three women prophets, Miriam, Deborah, and Huldah, serve as foremothers for Anna, the prophet.

In Exodus 15:20, the author describes Miriam, the older sister of Moses and Aaron, as a prophet: "Then the *prophet* Miriam...." Miriam leads the women with tambourines, song, and dance as all celebrate the victory over Pharaoh's army and their deliverance from slavery. Thus, she represents two important points: the first woman prophet mentioned in the Bible and the first woman to lead a nationalistic movement to new heights in the development of God's people. According to Judges 4:4, the prophet Deborah had two major roles in her leadership of the tribes: prophet and judge: "At that time Deborah, a *prophet*, wife of Lappidoth, was judging Israel." Interestingly, Deborah received the office of prophet from God and the office of judge by the will of the people. As prophet and judge, Deborah functioned as tribal chief. Her qualities of wisdom, foresight, and fearlessness brought her people to a more secure place in the land of Canaan. Because of her prophetic direction, the tribes enjoyed peace for many years. Huldah represents another woman prophet. In 2 Kings 22:14, King Josiah sought her counsel "so the priest Hilkiah, Ahikam, Achbor, Shaphan and Asaiah went to Huldah the *prophet*...where they consulted her." Along the same thoughts, 2 Chronicles 34:22 also confirms Huldah with the divinely chosen office of prophet: "So Hilkiah and those whom the king had sent went to the *prophet* Hulda...and spoke to her." Like all true prophets, Huldah does not back away from speaking the truth. She humbly, yet boldly proclaims what needs to be said. Her words as well as her divinely focused life brought Judah to new heights as a nation.

Anna is the only woman prophet in the third Gospel and reminds us of the respected women prophets from the Hebrew Bible. Luke 2:36–38 indicates that Anna had been widowed only seven years after her marriage. From that time onward, she spent her life in prayer and fasting. Luke also describes her as elderly, which suggests that Anna would have acquired a rich inner wisdom from her commitment to God. When Anna saw the infant Jesus, she began to prophesy "about the child to all who were looking for the redemption of Jerusalem" (Luke 2:38). Thus, the aged

Anna, the prophet, declares that the child would be the long-awaited Messiah.

Within the Lukan writings, the concept of "prophet" maintains a prominent position. The Gospel of Luke as well as the Acts of the Apostles uses the prophet motif as a major theme for Jesus as well as his disciples after the resurrection. Within this schema, Anna the prophet serves as a bridge between the prophets who have come before her in the Hebrew Bible and the prophets of Jesus that will come after the resurrection. As her name Anna the "favored one" implies, she gifts others with her wisdom and foresight. Truly, Anna becomes a model prophet for both Luke and Acts.

32. In Luke 2:49, after the child Jesus is separated from his family, why does he sound so disrespectful to his mother when they finally find him?

It seems most likely that Luke used this unique story to bridge the gap between Jesus' birth and his adulthood. At the beginning of the story, the evangelist states clearly that Jesus "was twelve years old" when the incident occurred. Traditionally, twelve-year-old Jewish boys engage in a bar mitzvah, which signifies a step to adulthood and dedication to religion. Therefore, the missing *child* from Nazareth replies as an *adult* to his mother in the Jerusalem temple. In double-tiered language, Jesus asserts that he needs to work for his Father, meaning God, not Joseph. His verbal intimacy in his connection with the Divine would have alarmed his parents and rabbis hearing the remark. His question, "did you not know" implies that his parents should have known. Yet, they do not. While the mission of Jesus unfolds before him, his parents do not seem to be privy to the plans. His mysterious reproach leaves Mary speechless, as she "treasured all these things in her heart" (Luke 2:51).

At the conclusion of the story (Luke 2:51–52), Luke relates that Jesus went back to Nazareth with them and "was obedient to them." Furthermore, as in the case of any human being, Jesus "increased in wisdom and stature." Essentially, Luke sets the stage for the development of Jesus from childhood to adulthood and a transition in Jesus' human as well as theological development. The stressful exchange between mother and son also allows the reader to sense the tension that so often exists in the maturing process between child and parent.

33. In Luke 6:13–16, the Twelve were chosen. If women accompanied Jesus and supported his ministry, why could they not have been commissioned as part of the Twelve?

In Luke 6:13–16, the evangelist describes the selection of twelve men to be named apostles out of a broader selection of disciples who followed Jesus. The designation of "twelve" comes from Mark 3:14, who also describes the appointment of twelve men as apostles. Yet, both Mark and Luke do not agree on the same names of the Twelve nor do they include women in their lists. However, other New Testament texts have a broader notion of the term "apostle." For example, apostle in the letters of Paul includes women such as Junia, who is named an apostle in Romans 16:7. Moreover, the later Gospel of John does not even use the term "apostle" to designate those chosen by Jesus. Instead, in the fourth Gospel the word "disciple" becomes interchangeable with apostle. In the third Gospel, however, Luke restricts the number to twelve and only considers men (Luke 6:13–15). Interestingly enough, in Acts 1:13–14, when the same author again provides a list of men who serve as apostles, he adds immediately that women had been actively involved within the group. Yet, Luke did not go as far as to identify them as apostles.

In effect, to limit the understanding of the term "apostle" to twelve men represents only the writings of the first three Gospel writers (Mark, Matthew, and Luke) and not those of Paul or John. This narrower representation of apostleship downplays equally important biblical texts that portray a much more inclusive description of apostle. In light of the need for a broader interpretation, the Roman Catholic Church in 1969 designated Mary of Magdala as *apostola apstolorum* ("apostle to the apostles"). In sum, an incorrect narrow interpretation of apostle ignores other biblical texts as well as prevents women from serving in leadership roles within some Christian churches.

34. What kind of deed would the woman in Luke 7:36–50 have committed that caused her to be identified as a sinner?

In Luke 7:37, the author identifies the female character as "a woman in the city, who was a sinner. . . . " Here it needs to be noted that the verb *was* (Greek, *en*) is in the imperfect mode in Greek, which can be translated, "who *used to be* a sinner." Later, in Luke 7:41–43, 47, the story indicates that the caring woman has already been forgiven by Jesus. Her love follows her divine forgiveness. Therefore, she stands as a model of gratitude for all that God has done for her.

Now, to your question, "what kind of deed" would the woman have engaged in to be called a sinner? In this story, Luke never mentions the nature of her past sin. While women in the first century CE usually remained in the private space of the home, historical evidence shows that some worked and traveled in the public space usually reserved for men, for example, if they worked in purple dye factories, served in health care, or traveled. Financially desperate women would have to beg or become prostitutes. Subsequently, they could have had contact with unacceptable people, such as, non-Jews, undesirable items, such as, ritually unclean foods, and places, such as, Gentile homes. All these would render a woman unclean or having "sin."

35. In Luke 7:36–50, a woman from the city enters a Pharisee's home and interrupts dinner to anoint the feet of Jesus with oils from an alabaster jar. Why does Luke identify only the woman in the story as a sinner?

The question of "why" Luke identifies *only* the woman as a sinner has no direct answer. In a broader context, why does Luke even mention someone who had sinned in the past at all? The answer appears in Luke's use of two prominent themes that emerge throughout the Gospel and Acts, namely, the title of Jesus as Prophet and his ability to forgive sins. In these works, Luke adopts the Greek term, *aphesis*, which means "release/freedom" to represent the greatest freedom that God can offer, namely, "forgiveness of sins." These two themes of "prophet" and "forgiveness of sins" are juxtaposed throughout Luke–Acts. Both appear in this multilevel, lengthy narrative.

In 7:47, when Jesus proclaims that the woman's past sins had been forgiven and even repeats this divine action in 7:48, he acts and speaks as prophet. In both verses, Luke employs a form of the Greek word, *aphesis*, to translate the phrase, "forgiveness of sins." Luke, therefore, portrays Jesus as more than an ordinary biblical prophet.

While the woman generously pours expensive ointment on his feet, washes them, dries them, and kisses them, she acts with an attitude of deep gratitude and open heart. Here the woman, rather than Simon, acts as host. Customarily, it remained the responsibility of the host to have the feet of the guests washed and to kiss the guest in a welcome gesture. Yet this rude host neglected to give Jesus either sign of welcome. Unlike the resentful Simon and his disbelieving guests, this openhearted woman, through her unusual generous actions, radiates a deep love and commitment to Jesus. In effect, this narrative spotlights the outpouring of a woman's grateful love, as well as the themes of Jesus as prophet and his ability to forgive sins.

36. In Luke 7:36–50, although nothing is said about the nature of the woman's sins, why do some assume this woman was a prostitute? How did this nameless woman who anointed Jesus and is seen as a sinner become connected to Mary Magdalene? How did Mary Magdalene become identified with prostitution?

It is true that nothing in the story names any past sin of the woman or even identifies her as a prostitute. How then, did the identification of the unnamed woman with the figure of Mary of Magdala and prostitution happen? While no direct indication of sexual misconduct has been made, some interpreters suggest that Luke's description of her as "a woman in the city" seems suspect and implies otherwise. For them, her touching Jesus' feet could also be construed as an erotic gesture. Their comments reinforce the traditional assumption that this woman was a prostitute. However, nowhere does the text suggest such direct or even indirect statements.

It helps to look at the placement of this story within the Gospel and briefly look at the historical development of this passage within Christianity. Contextually, this narrative precedes Luke 8:1–3, where Mary of Magdala tops a list of some women disciples of Jesus. Ordinarily in biblical lists, the first name honors the most important figure. By placing Mary of Magdala in that position, Luke recognizes her important status both during the ministry of Jesus and later within the Christian communities.

However, Luke's placement of the two stories side by side has led later ecclesiastical authorities to conflate the two biblical figures of the unnamed woman and Mary of Magdala and draw improper conclusions. This incorrect reading misrepresents the two major women figures in both stories in that they have been combined into one person, namely, Mary of Magdala. Western Christianity assumed that Mary of Magdala lived as a sinner and worked as a prostitute. Jane Schaeberg calls the damaging conflation "an extremely important distortion in the imagination of Western

Christianity" ("Luke," in *WBC*, 374). No biblical evidence exists to conflate Mary of Magdala with the unknown woman who had once sinned, or with any act of prostitution. This biased portrayal damages a true reading of the sacred text.

Most significantly, it harms the portrait of Mary of Magdala and her apostolic authority within the Church. This last point is very important because it has had a negative effect on leadership roles for women in certain Christian churches since that time. As Rosemary Radford Ruether notes, "the tradition of Mary Magdalene as a sinner was developed in orthodox (western) Christianity primarily to displace the apostolic authority claimed for women through her name" (*Women-Church*, 286 n. 1).

37. In Luke 8:1–3, if women gave up their wealth to follow Jesus, why weren't they given leadership roles in the early Church?

On the contrary, women did function in authoritative positions in the early Church, as demonstrated by some of the authentic letters of Paul. Named women such as Chloe, Prisca, Euodia, Syntyche, Apphia, and Phoebe were leaders associated with Pauline communities. However, the first three Gospels may reflect a strain between women leaders and a Petrine, male-oriented leadership. For example, the Gospels of Mark and Matthew do not even include women like Mary of Magdala until the crucifixion and burial scenes at end of their Gospels. While Luke includes some women disciples early in Luke 8, he reduces their role to financial supporters and fails to mention their active roles of leadership in the public arena. Francine Cardman notes that, "as Church orders appealed to apostolic authority rather than the authority of Paul... they began to change the patterns of power and the nature of leadership in the churches" ("Women, Ministry and Church Order in Early Christianity," in *Women & Christian Origins*, 308).

Within the ecclesiastical political struggle for authority and Christianity's acceptance into the Roman Empire in the latter half of the first century CE, Luke attempted to make the Gospel more acceptable to Greco-Roman converts by limiting the historical portrait of women as speakers and leaders. Luke 8:1–3 illustrates this type of description. To his credit, Luke clearly places women with Jesus throughout his Galilean ministry. He also presents a list of women and rightly puts Mary of Magdala at the head of the list.

However, Luke offers an imperfect picture of the women by identifying them as "some women who had been cured of evil spirits and infirmities…." (Luke 8:2). Such characterizations about the women, attempting to diminish their authority with such unnecessary descriptions, appear only in the Gospel of Luke.

38. It seems in the first century women and men led very segregated lives. How could unaccompanied women have been allowed to follow Jesus, as in Luke 8:1–3?

In the first-century Mediterranean world, men and women often lived segregated lives. The thought of Jesus traveling with women from village to village throughout Galilee raises issues of scandal. Jane Schaberg offers a possible solution through rhetorical inquiry. She questions whether the geography of Galilee, which had villages near each other, may have provided the opportunity for the women to travel by day and return to their homes at night. Furthermore, she asks that since Luke describes disciples of Jesus traveling in pairs (Luke 10), could not the women have traveled in pairs or with another male? ("Luke," in *WBC*, 375).

These comments provide something of a solution to your question. While no direct textual evidence exists, it does seem strange, as Schaberg indicates, that Luke presents no evidence of dishonor that resulted from the travel habits of these women with Jesus and the others. Since Luke projects the theme of "joy" throughout his two volumes, would he omit any trace of scandal, even scandal without just cause?

39. In Luke 8:1–3, what is the significance of naming Joanna and Suzanna? Was Joanna *the wife of Herod's steward Chuza* or was that a fourth unnamed woman in the list?

Naming these women gives credibility to them. It also demonstrates that they remained very important to the traditions of the Lukan communities. The first name, Joanna, immediately follows Mary of Magdala, the most important name on the list. Therefore, Joanna also ranked high in ministerial activities among the early churches. In Luke 24:10, her name appears again when the evangelist describes the faithful women at the tomb. Furthermore, when Luke speaks of the women followers of Galilee at both the death (Luke 23:49) and burial (Luke 23:55) of Jesus, Joanna would have been among them.

In this text, Joanna is identified as the wife of Chuza, Herod's steward. The Greek, *epitropus*, (steward) denotes a "manager" (Luke T. Johnson, *The Gospel of Luke*, 131) within the governing system of Herod Antipas. As one of the sons of the famed Herod the Great, he reigned over Galilee and Peraea. Subsequently, both Joanna and her husband would have had contact with the ruling classes and influential wealthy families of Galilee. As a member of the higher social class, Joanna may have supported Jesus not only financially, but within her social circles as well.

In general, both these named and unnamed women functioned as more than companions to Jesus and the others. They were close friends and faithful followers of Jesus during his Galilean ministry.

40. In Luke 8:3, what resources might these women have had that they so willingly shared with Jesus and the disciples? Weren't women of that time chattel who owned nothing?

Luke indicates in 8:3 that particular women who traveled with Jesus and others "provided for them out of their resources."

The verse offers two significant points in the original Greek. The Greek term for "resources," *hyparchonton*, translates into "money," "possessions," and/or "property." The more important phrase "provided for them" comes from Mark 15:41 to describe the women as patrons/benefactors. The English translation "provided for" (Greek, *diakoneo*), means "to serve." The noun, *deacon*, originates from the same Greek stem. Your remark about ancient women having no financial resources needs some qualifications. Some biblical texts, such as, Luke 8:3, suggest that women could be financially solvent in the Greco-Roman world of the first century. Later in Acts 16:14, Luke describes Lydia of Thyatira as a "dealer" in purple dye cloth. He also presents her as head of a household. A few chapters later in Acts 18:3, Luke narrates that Priscilla, along with her husband, worked in the trade of tent-making. These Lukan references portray certain women as financially independent, or at least equal in business. Thus, the women that Luke names in Luke 8:2–3 exemplify some of the best practices of religious Jewish women. They do good works and provide generously for others in need.

41. In Luke 8:19–21, why does Jesus sound so stern when Mary and his brothers come to see him?

In Luke 8:19–21, the remarks of Jesus may seem quite harsh to any reader of the Gospel. This story describes a visit to Jesus by "his mother and his brothers." In the narrative, the family "comes and seeks" Jesus. They seem to stand at the crossroads between family members and disciples. When Jesus proclaims that "My mother and my brothers are those who hear the word of God and do it" (Luke 8:21), he extends the call of discipleship to his mother and family.

Jesus' remarks about family ties break the notion of the family as a person's primary identity and support system. This notion would have been unthinkable in the first century because all honor, occupation, status, and social position stemmed from the family to which one was born. Now the new family of believers overrides the birth family and forms new bonds of kinship (Robert Tannehill, *Luke*, 143–44). The family of God, which reaches far beyond physical family ties, joins in following the word of God. Later, in Acts 1:14, Luke narrates that "Mary, the mother of Jesus, as well as his brothers" met with the others in the upper room. According to Luke, then, Jesus' birth family did respond to the invitation because they ranked among the early disciples who believed in him.

42. In Luke 10:41, why does Jesus correct Martha for wanting a little help in the kitchen? Weren't there others, including men, available to help feed Jesus and his party?

When you look more closely at this special Lukan pronouncement story in 10:38–42, you will notice that nowhere does the text refer to a kitchen, meals, table, or food. However, many have mistakenly viewed the narrative as a meal story. To see if Jesus really "corrects Martha," it is important to understand Luke's purpose in relating this offensive remark. Luke places the Martha and Mary story in Luke 10 as part of the travel narrative in which Jesus journeys to Jerusalem as a prophet to be murdered. Within the chapter, the stories of the appointed seventy disciples sent out to minister, the parable of the Good Samaritan, and the dialogue with the Jewish lawyer appear consecutively. Thus, the theme of discipleship surfaces as one of the major themes throughout the chapter. Discipleship includes being chosen, listening to the voice of God and to the needs of others, as well as serving them with an open heart.

In Luke 10:41, Jesus replies to Martha's previous request and observes that Martha appears "worried and distracted "about much service (*diakonian*)." Here the evangelist makes use of the Greek term, *diakonian* for "service." Through a careful word study, John N. Collins (*Diakonia: Re-Interpreting the Ancient Sources*, 73–191) has demonstrated that in ancient times the term seldom appeared in texts. Furthermore, the word does not usually refer to waiting on tables, but describes one authorized to perform a role or task. This person acts as a mediator for another person. In early Christian communities, the person led the community as a representative of Christ.

Accordingly, when Luke describes Martha's service as *diakonian*, he portrays Martha in a very important role of "leader" within the context of later household Churches. Leadership encompasses preaching and ministry according to Luke's frequent use of *diakonia* in Acts of the Apostles. If Martha's distress in 10:40 is viewed in the light of such leadership, her concern reflects the performance of her duties as a person in charge. She represents one who ministers, preaches, and supports others. In addition, her sister, Mary, would be seen as a partner in this leadership not only as family, but also in an ecclesial sense. If a partnership in leadership falters, the entire community suffers.

Martha's plea may arouse emotions, especially among women, because of their unheard voices and cries for justice throughout Church history. In this framework, the words of Jesus may sound dismissive. However, throughout this entire story, does the situation reflect the thoughts of Jesus or those of the evangelist many years later, trying to reposition women in the more submissive and silent role of listener? Looking carefully at other Lukan texts about women, it appears as if this story represents the evangelist's time, rather than the time of the historical Jesus.

43. What point was the evangelist trying to make with regard to a woman's place in relation to Jesus and ancient culture?

While ancient culture, both in the Greco-Roman world as well as in the Gentile Christian communities, allowed periodically some formal education of women, the general trend at this time would have been to keep women's involvement in the public sphere restricted. Accordingly, this remarkable story of Martha and Mary reflects the evangelist's attempt to make this Gospel "acceptable" to Greco-Roman society at large by placing the receptiveness of Mary over the actions of Martha.

44. In Luke 10:42, what is the *one thing* that Jesus tells Martha is needed?

Any careful study of the history of Luke 10:42 reveals that this text proved difficult to understand. In the early years of transmission of the text, many variants had been made by scribes who copied this Greek text in order to clarify its meaning. However, I shall focus on the accepted and older variant, which reads "There is need of only one thing."

The "one thing" in verse 42 refers to the chosen activity of Mary, that of listening to the word of Jesus, a choice that will provide spiritual nourishment for her. During the transfiguration scene that occurs one chapter earlier, the Divine voice from heaven declares to the chosen three apostles "This is my Son, my Chosen, *listen to him!*" (9:35). This command to remain attentive to the prophetic voice also reminds the reader of Moses' promise of a new prophet after his death, one whom "you will *heed (listen to)*" (Deut 18:15). With the qualifier "one thing," the evangelist emphasizes "listening" to the voice of Jesus over active engagement at this moment.

45. In Luke 10:42, Jesus says, "Mary has chosen the better part." What does that mean? Wasn't it selfish of Mary not to help her sister so that Martha could also visit with Jesus?

The remainder of verse 42 declares that "Mary has chosen the good (*agathen*) part" (my translation). Unfortunately, many translators use the words "better part" which overemphasizes her role as receptive pupil. The "good part" for Luke translates into Mary as passive learner. Her voice remains silent. Despite this preference for Luke, the remainder of the verse does not disqualify Martha's position (*diakonian*), as has already been discussed in Question 42. In this story, Martha is already serving others. In the only two stories about her (Luke 10:38–42; John 11:1–44), she functions as the head of the household.

You question the selfishness of Mary, but this story does not reflect any historical confrontation between two sisters. Rather, this verse attempts to minimize the authority of Martha as a leader with a voice and to promote the submissiveness of Mary without one. Unfortunately, the Gospel of Luke and some of the pastoral letters have been interpreted in such a way that silenced women and minimized their roles as decision makers within the churches. As a result, texts such as "Mary has chosen the good part" have generated anguish and heated discussion in the lives of women for many years.

While Luke may have attempted to minimize the active role of women in leadership, the outcome would not have been what he expected. Actually, the phrase, the "good part" has another side to it and in this case, a positive one. Here the Lukan Jesus encourages women to learn. By being a student and listening to the word of the Lord, the theological education of women has been promoted. This divine calling to grow theologically through education, leads to knowledge, wisdom, and leadership. Therefore, this seemingly harmful text has failed to thwart the intention of the Divine, which empowers both women and men equally.

46. In Luke 13:10–17, why does Jesus heal the crippled woman in the synagogue when she simply appears but does not expressly ask for healing?

This powerful Lukan miracle story represents the second of three accounts that describes Jesus healing on the Sabbath with controversial results (compare with 6:6–11; 14:1–6). Within this narrative in 13:10–17, the evangelist indicates that an unnamed woman who came to the synagogue to pray has been crippled for eighteen years from a "spirit." The "spirit" of sickness has caused her to walk "bent over" for numerous years and thus severely limited her physical activity. Illness usually causes physical weakness, which leads to a restricted life. Since people did not live very long in the first century, "eighteen years" of incapacity represents a major portion of her life.

When Jesus saw the predicament of this woman, he called her over, spoke to her, laid his hands on her, and healed her. The unnamed woman immediately responds with words of praise to God. This powerful encounter aroused great indignation in the leader of the synagogue. Instead of joining his voice to the chorus of praise, he resents the marvelous moment of divine action that brought joy and wholeness to the grateful woman.

Often, gifted moments of the Divine will be unanticipated or not requested. The need to be grateful for these blessings is one of the clear lessons from this healing narrative. We do not always ask God for the frequent opportunities for growth and wholeness that grace our lives, but we need to welcome the unexpected, even though it may not be what we had envisioned.

In this story, the unnamed bent-over woman still came to the synagogue to pray to God for a variety of reasons. She demonstrates no bitterness. The fact that she praised God as her first response gives the reader a clue into her life in general. Unlike the religious leader, who will later complain about Jesus' great gift of healing to her, she offered praises to God, despite her painful condition. Thus, we encounter a woman filled with gratitude for however God allowed her life to be.

The physically healthy religious leader holds onto his resentment in the guise of external observance to Sabbath law. Even though Sabbath law was intended to free people to celebrate the weekly feast, the synagogue leader was very displeased over the physical freedom given to the handicapped woman. Consequently, he who has been chosen to lead others to spiritual enrichment fails miserably in his position. His angry attitude opens a chasm between himself and the marvelous deed of Jesus. In effect, the miracle story develops into a controversy about human power and divine authority. In the end, even the people rejected the pompous, resentful attitude of the so-called leader and "rejoiced" at the healing of the woman and the action of Jesus. Unlike this religious leader, the woman displays her thankfulness, wisdom, and hope in the God of surprises.

47. In Luke 15:8–10, why would the woman who lost and found only one silver coin call her friends and neighbors to celebrate? What was the significance of this coin?

This brief parable found only in the Gospel of Luke appears as one of three consecutive narratives about the theme of being lost and finally found. To answer your question about why one silver coin would become a cause for celebration, we need to recognize that the woman's meticulous search must be viewed on more than one level. On a human level, a poor woman who lost even one coin would search assiduously for it because it could be used to pay some debt like rent, food, or clothing. The loss of it seriously impacted her living situation.

Since many dwellings of the poor in first-century Palestine lacked any natural light from windows, her broom and lamp would help her to find the coin, which may have fallen on a dark dirt floor. Finally, having found the lost coin after a long hunt, the woman calls friends and neighbors to celebrate. On a theological level, God, like the woman, searches for someone who has been lost in life. When that person responds and finds a way back to the Divine, this outcome would be cause for great celebration.

48. In Luke 18:1–8, why would the judge refuse the persistent widow's pleas for justice?

This Lukan parable describes a judge, who has been characterized as "unjust." Ideally, any person who attained the position of judge, would have both good leadership and integrity. Unfortunately, this judge lacks both qualities. From Luke's brief description, he appears deficient in respect and honesty for everyone. As a result, he has no concern for the plight of the poor, especially women, who were dismissed as lacking credibility by the customs of ancient societies.

Despite his disregard for everyone, the poor persistent widow came to him repeatedly for help. She would not lose heart in her pursuit for justice against her opponent. As such, she offers the reader a magnificent lesson in hope. Like the persistent widow, who never lost her zest for justice despite the repeated refusal on the part of the uncaring judge, we, too, need to be diligent in our journey of faith. As she would not stop her pleas to a shameless judge, we need to believe that our caring and loving God does hear our requests, despite any injustices that we witness along the way.

49. In Luke 18:1–8, what kind of justice granted by God does Luke refer to in the parable of the persistent widow?

At the conclusion of the parable (verses 6–8), Jesus explains its meaning in terms of justice for those who seek it. In contrasting the unjust judge with God, Jesus proclaims that God "will quickly grant justice" (verse 8). Justice in this parable refers to long-term fidelity in the ways of God. At the time of this writing in the late first century CE, Christians expected the imminent return of the risen Jesus, but it proved to be an extended wait. In this vein, the Lukan Jesus tries to assure them to be patient and persistent in their belief that God does hear their prayer. We, like the early Christians, need to be more like the persistent widow. Although as a widow she represents one of the most vulnerable of all society, her courageous stance with the unscrupulous judge makes her one of the strongest. The widow's boundless hope and courage in the pursuit of justice makes her the victor in this powerful parable.

50. In Luke 20:27–33, why would a woman wish to marry her deceased husband's brother in order to have children counted as her deceased husband's? Did widows have to do this?

The example of the widow marrying her deceased husband's brother does not necessarily reflect the wishes of the woman because she had little or no freedom in the situation. Remember that after a young woman left her father's home because of an arranged marriage, she moved from being the property of her father to the property of her husband. In this respect, she had no choices. If her husband died, she became the property of her husband's family. In the case of this widow, the ancient Mosaic law of the levirate marriage would apply, which actually helped the woman to cement her place in ancient Jewish society.

This levirate law in Deuteronomy 25:5–6 states "when brothers reside together, and one of them dies and has no son, the wife of the deceased shall not be married outside the family to a stranger. Her husband's brother shall go in to her, taking her in marriage, and performing the duty of a husband's brother to her, and the firstborn whom she bears shall succeed to the name of the deceased brother, so that his name may not be blotted out of Israel." In later ancient Jewish writings, the practical minutiae appear in the Mishnah tractate *Yebamoth 1:14*. In many ways, the widow would want to do this in order to honor her dead husband and his descendants, to provide financial stability for herself and her child, as well as to bring honor to herself, her husband, and both families.

51. In Luke 21:1–4, why would the poor widow put all she had to live on into the treasury? What is the treasury? Does this mean the woman goes without food and shelter? If so, how is this commendable behavior?

The brief story in Luke 21 carries a strong message. It contrasts the degree of sacrifice between the donations of the wealthy and the poor as they contribute to the treasury within the Jerusalem temple. At the time of Jesus the temple contained three inner courts. The one situated on the eastern side has been identified as the Court of the Women. The temple treasury was located within this court. According to the *Mishnah, m.Shek 5:6*, the treasury represented the location where "the devout used to put their gifts in secret and the poor of good families receive support there from in secret." In ancient society, a widow without sons to provide food and shelter for her would have to beg for her livelihood and, therefore, it would be unwise for the woman to give "all she had to live on" (Luke 21:4) to the treasury. When Jesus suggests that she gave much more than the wealthy, does he applaud her actions? Scholars have debated this point without coming to a consensus. Some, for example, concentrate on the astonishing value of the gift in the eyes of God and defend the generosity of the poor, who provide life to others by sharing all that they have.

Other scholars, however, view this story as a lament over a religious system that devours the livelihood of the poor. They suggest that the words of Jesus imply a condemnation of the temple treasury because it represents a system that takes from the poor. Furthermore, by proclaiming divine legitimacy, it forces a religious requirement on the poor that they cannot meet without becoming victims of grave injustice.

In this light, Jesus does not praise the actions of this poor widow. Rather, he condemns unfair religious laws that abuse God's people. To support this view, we need to understand the context of this brief story. Jesus' words about the poor widow follow another warning in the preceding chapter. In Luke 20:45–47, Jesus warns the people to be careful of religious leaders who "devour widows' houses and for the sake of appearance say long prayers" (Luke 20:47). Here, then, he continues his criticism of a religious system that exploits the impoverished, especially unprotected women.

52. In Luke 23:27, if many people followed Jesus to his crucifixion, why are only unnamed women mentioned as "beating their breasts and wailing for him"?

Luke 23 continues the cruel last days of Jesus' life on earth, namely, his trial and death. This chapter embodies a public world of male religious and political figures who mock, humiliate, and murder him by crucifixion. This was one of the most degrading forms of execution in the Roman Empire and was a common form of punishment for non-Roman citizens because it produced fear in the bystanders and makes *pax romana* (peace of Rome) more attainable. Despite all the public display of hatred toward Jesus in chapter 23, Luke's mention of the "women of Jerusalem" brings a refreshing moment of positive support and fidelity toward him.

Unlike the male disciples of Jesus, who Luke never mentions in this painful scene, the faithful women reinforce their deep loyalty and compassion toward Jesus by "beating their breasts and wailing for him." Weeping was customary at an ancient funeral. Here their verbal actions anticipate the end as Jesus moves toward the place of execution amidst jeering Roman soldiers and restless crowds. These brave and faithful women represent all who grieve the horrible fate of Jesus on his way to the crucifixion.

53. In Luke 23:28–29, what does Jesus mean when he says to the women that the days will come when they will say, "Blessed are the barren, and the wombs that never bore, and the breasts that never nursed"? Weren't fertility and childbearing very important to the Jewish people? Why is Jesus blessing the barren?

This surprising blessing coming from the mouth of Jesus could confuse any reader. Traditionally, in biblical texts, barrenness would not be seen as a blessing (Gen 11:30; 25:21; 29:31; Judg

13:2; Luke 1:7). On the contrary, children brought wealth to families in many ways, such as honoring parents by being descendants, assisting in the family business, aiding the parents in their old age, and so on.

However, Jesus' blessing praises barrenness instead of child-bearing. Why? This praise has roots in Isaiah 54:1, with the acclamation "Sing, O barren one...," the prophet praises barrenness during the Judahites' imprisonment in Babylon. Likewise, the Lukan warning in 23:29 reaches beyond the meaning of one woman. Here we must consider that the blessing, "blessed are the barren..." represents the thoughts of Luke, who wrote after the destruction of Jerusalem by the Romans. In this light, the comment blesses those whose barrenness spared children from acute suffering and death from the terrible destruction in 70 CE. Roman forces entered Jerusalem, destroyed the second temple, burned the city to the ground, and exiled the Jews. The destruction of war brings a very heavy burden especially to women and children. Subsequently, Jesus urges the women not to lament for him, but for themselves and their children.

54. In Luke 23:49, could women of this time actually follow Jesus all the way from Galilee without fear of scorn or scandal?

It is very possible that the women feared scorn or scandal in their roles as disciples. During the first century CE, the expected role of women differed from that of men. As I have stated previously, women remained under the authority of their fathers until marriage, when they became property of their husbands. Moreover, often they did not have the freedom to travel as men did. Even though these women may have been more emancipated than their female ancestors, they still lacked equality with men.

In this social mind-set, women followers traveling with men who were not their husbands would have seemed strange to onlookers. In this case, the faithful women disciples could have been the targets of scorn throughout their travels. This point only underlines the cost of their discipleship in following Jesus. Now, as Jesus dies painfully on the cross, the safety of these same women becomes even more imperiled. As Galileans, they would have been viewed as outsiders by Jerusalemites. As women attending a public Roman crucifixion, they would have put themselves in danger. Their continued support of the brutalized Jesus as he dies on Golgotha demonstrates that their committed discipleship far exceeds any fear of bodily harm. Finally, their presence in the text leads to their next task, that of anointing and preparing the body of Jesus for burial.

55. Luke 23:55–56 describes the application of spices and ointments for the ritual of burial. Was it usually performed by women? If so, why was it acceptable for women to become ritually unclean by touching the dead, but not for men?

The faithful women disciples remained with Jesus even after his death. The text indicates that both the women and Joseph of Arimathea touched the corpse of Jesus, which made them all unclean. Ritual cleanliness did not have to do with sin, but with religious fittingness. The unclean would be made clean through a religious ritual, depending on the cause of their impurity.

Presumably, an executed criminal would not always have had a proper burial. Therefore, the work of Joseph of Arimathea and the preparation of Jesus' body by these faithful women took both fore-sight and bravery. Their daring actions had great risks. For example, they could have brought suspicion on themselves by both Roman and Jewish authorities who could have hurt them through accusations or even imprisonment.

Moreover, as witnesses of the events that led to his death, the women saw a chain of evidence in the final events of Jesus' life. Only they could relate specifics about the events of the crucifixion and the place of the tomb. This demonstrates that these women witnesses were truly committed disciples of Jesus. Their heroic leadership is a great example to fellow disciples.

56. In Luke 24:11–12, why didn't the male apostles believe the women when they were told that Jesus was alive? Why did they have to go and see for themselves?

In Luke 24:1–10, the women are the first witnesses to the empty tomb and the ones selected to hear the message about the risen Jesus from the divine messengers. In turn, they related all that they had seen and heard to the disciples. Unfortunately, in 24:11 we learn that the other disciples did not believe them: "But these words seemed to them an idle tale (*leros*) and they did not believe them." The Greek word, *leros*, which can be translated as "nonsense," carries the sense of hysteria from a delirious person. Therefore, Luke's use of the term, *leros*, is quite condescending.

Your question as to "why" the men disciples dismissed the women's story has no direct answer since we do not know the thoughts of these men. However, as I have mentioned before, women would not have been considered credible witnesses in any religious or political court in the first century CE. Interestingly, only Luke's Gospel relates such resistance to the women's message.

In the next Lukan story of the two disciples on the road to Emmaus, you will notice that the risen Jesus reprimands the mistrust of the men disciples toward the words of the women disciples (Luke 24:22–25). When the travelers told Jesus about the morning's event and how they did not believe what the women had told them, Jesus reprimands their disbelief beginning with, "Oh, how foolish you are." God's choice of women in the resurrection scene proves to be intentional and cannot be disbelieved or ignored.

Jesus continues chiding them with "and how slow of heart to believe all that the prophets had declared" (24:25). In this scene, "the prophets" to whom Jesus refers indicates the faithful women disciples who have declared the divine message earlier that day, but whom the male disciples refused to believe. In this case, Jesus' rebuke of male priority over God's choice of women to proclaim the divine message reemphasizes the place of women in the divine order and secures the role of women in the affairs of God.

57. In Luke 24:13–19, regarding the journey to Emmaus, could one of the disciples on the road have been a woman? Could they have been a couple?

In recent years, many have questioned the gender of the unknown traveler in the resurrection appearance on the road to Emmaus. While 24:18 identifies one as Cleopas, a man's name, the other person has not been identified. However, in the dialogue with Jesus, Luke indicates that they both reply and identify with the male disciples who did not believe the account of the women (24:19–24). Such dismissal of the women's story seems to indicate that both travelers were male. On the other hand, if one person had been the wife of Cleopas, the response in the text could reflect a response by the husband alone, who would speak for the family as head of the household. Unfortunately, the text does not provide real evidence to your question. Therefore, a true answer remains unknown.

Chapter 5

The Gospel of John

58. In John 2, at the wedding in Cana, did Mary know that the time had come for Jesus to start his ministry?

I suggest that the answer is "No." When "the mother of Jesus" seems to ignore Jesus' statement "My hour has not yet come" in 2:4, she shows that she has no knowledge of the divine plan for her son in this Gospel. In John, the "hour" indicates God's time and climaxes in the moment of Jesus' crucifixion, death, and glory. Consequently, the moment of action for Jesus cannot be controlled by human time. Clearly, the "mother of Jesus" does not understand this. Since there have been no miracles thus far in this Fourth Gospel, the "mother of Jesus" would not expect one. Rather, her implied request illustrates a deep trust that her son will somehow prevent the pain and shame of the hosting families.

Jesus *does* listen to his mother and alleviate the embarrassing situation for the bridal families. The resulting abundance of the finest wine restores honor to the families by guaranteeing no shortage of drink will occur. Furthermore, the top quality of wine indicates the wealth and the financial support of family and friends for this wedding. On the divine level, the abundance of wine reflects the theme of Deutero-Isaiah 54:4–8, 62:4–5, where the theme of the wedding feast anticipates messianic times of celebration and joy.

59. In John 2:4, Jesus refers to his mother as "*Woman*." Isn't that disrespectful?

For a twenty-first-century reader, the address of Jesus to his mother appears harsh in John 2:4. The title, *woman*, sounds abrasive. Today, anyone speaking this way would seem crass and bad-mannered. In first-century Palestine, however, using the word *woman* (*gyne*) was not impolite, rude, or a rebuke of any kind. Rather, it shows Jesus' courteous way of addressing women (Matt 15:28; Luke 13:12; John 4:21; 13:10; 20:13). Today, however, the English language does not offer a nuanced equivalent of this Greek word.

In addition, references to Mary of Nazareth appear only twice in the Fourth Gospel, who has been described as the "mother of Jesus" (John 2:1; 19:25–26). In these stories, Jesus refers to his mother solely as "woman" (John 2:4; 19:26). These examples strengthen the position that Jesus had no intention of disrespecting his mother. Instead, he continues to honor her with the title, *woman*. Finally, his address, *woman* instead of *mother*, underlines the point that Jesus does not belong to Mary, but rather to God, his heavenly parent.

60. What would have happened to Jesus if the Pharisees had seen him talking to the Samaritan woman? What would have happened to the woman if she'd been caught?

This would have never happened. No Pharisee would have entered the defiled territory of Samaria and witnessed any such dialogue. They would go out of their way to avoid entering Samaritan territory in order to avoid defilement and the breach of any other Jewish religious laws.

Early in the narrative, the woman's question, "How is it that you, a Jew, ask a drink of me, a woman of Samaria?" in 4:9 indicates that the dialogue occurs under unusual, even scandalous, circumstances. When the Evangelist adds an explanation of the severity of the situation in the same verse, the offensiveness of the behavior is confirmed. Later, in 4:27, when the disciples seem shocked that Jesus speaks with a woman of Samaria, the reader knows well that the entire scene at the well reflects strange cultural and religious circumstances.

As for your question about the outcome if the woman had been "caught," in general, as a woman, she was not permitted to speak to men, especially strangers. As a Samaritan, she was forbidden to speak with Jews, above all, Jewish men. The point that she visited the well at noon, suggests that she had already been shunned by her neighbors. If they had seen her talking with a strange Jewish man, their ridicule of her would have increased, perhaps even to the point of excommunication from the village.

61. What was life like for Samaritan women? Who were the Samaritans, and why was Jesus trying to convert this woman from her own beliefs?

Samaritans were the product of intermarriage between ancient peoples from both the remnant northern tribes of Israel and prisoners of war from Assyrian conquests who had been sent to the territory of Samaria. As a result, their religious beliefs, practices, and traditions evolved so that they differed in areas from their Israelite roots and Jewish counterparts. The Samaritans believed only in the Torah, that is, the first five books of the Hebrew Bible. They dismissed the biblical prophets as inauthentic and held only one prophet, Moses, in the highest esteem. Life for Samaritan women would have been like that of other peasants in Palestine. The wife tended to all domestic duties, such as, childrearing, housekeeping, meal preparation, and laundry. If the family farmed, most likely the wife would work alongside her husband in times of planting and harvesting. Other times she kept to her duties in the private space in and around the home. Most first-century people were poor farmers. A woman from such a family would most likely never travel far from the village her entire life because of domestic duties, the cost of travel, and the expectation of society that women remain in the private space.

In the story, Jesus does not try to convert the unnamed woman. A conversion does take place because the woman responds to the words of Jesus with an open heart and mind. During the conversation, his request for a drink of water progresses to a discussion about the coming of the Messiah. This theological development enlivens both the hearts of the unnamed woman as well as Jesus. Unlike Nicodemus, who continues to doubt the words of Jesus in the preceding chapter, John 3, this woman of Samaria in John 4 questions him openly and fearlessly. Thus, she grows in divine wisdom and faith because of her honesty with Jesus. In this story, the rejected woman of Samaria exhibits much more faith than Nicodemus, the learned Jewish leader of Jerusalem. Due to her receptiveness, Jesus reveals himself to her. Thus, in the Gospel of John, belief in the person of Jesus supplants both the Samaritan and Jewish religious traditions.

62. In John 4:11–12, why is the Samaritan woman so skeptical about the source of the living water? What is living water?

Your question, "what is living water?" reflects how fortunate we are to have a good water supply available to us each day. On a human level, "living water" is water from a source, such as, a clean spring or mountain stream that flows and, therefore, cannot become stagnant. On a divine level, as in this story, "living water" signifies the gift of God that flows constantly in each one of us.

In this narrative, the conversation between Jesus and the unnamed woman takes place at the well of Jacob. Well water, which may include remnants of rain from months ago, contains still, "non-living" water. As you know from observing rain puddles, still water can become stagnant and even dangerous as a breeding place for insects, birds, and rodents with diseases.

Therefore, when Jesus offers the woman of Samaria, "living water," he offers her a gift beyond measure. In the Hebrew Bible, "living water" often represents a reflection of God's salvation in various prophetic writings (Isa 12:3; Ezek 47:1–12; Zech 14:8). Understandably, the woman does not immediately grasp Jesus' offer of "living water," which translates into a new life with God, and so she replies, "Sir (*kurie*), you have no bucket, and the well is deep. Where do you get that living water?" (4:11). In this instance, the woman and Jesus speak on two different levels, human and divine. Soon, however, the woman will understand the words of Jesus on the divine level, when he shares with her his identity as Messiah.

Unlike the disturbing conversation with Nicodemus in John 3, when Jesus became frustrated with his inability to be open to the divine word, here in John 4, the woman at the well has been quite openhearted from her initial encounter with Jesus. Throughout the story, Jesus recognizes her willingness to learn, her ability and ease in discussing religious matters, and her growing trust in him. Consequently, as the conversation continues, Jesus speaks to her about theological topics, from water "gushing up to eternal life," internal worship that occurs neither in Jerusalem nor on Mount Gerizim and finally, to his claim of messiahship.

63. In John 4, if the Samaritan woman was considered an outcast, why would anyone in the town believe her when she said, "He cannot be the Messiah, can he?"

For years, the unnamed woman of Samaria has been thought of as an outcast in different ways. As a woman, her thoughts and opinions would have been suspect or ignored. As a Samaritan, Jews would have regarded her as unclean and a heretic. Additionally, in the story, her own neighbors seemed to have cast her aside, which was why she came to the well at noon.

Yet after her marvelous dialogue with Jesus, this woman's humble risk taking, leadership skills, and intelligent maneuvering allow her to go to the villagers and invite them to "come and see" Jesus (4:29). Earlier, Jesus employs the phrase, "come and see" in 1:39 as an invitation to discipleship. Here the woman, as the only person in the Fourth Gospel to speak for Jesus during his ministry, offers her own townspeople the opportunity to become his disciples.

Since the woman realizes that they would refuse to listen to any direct form of good news about Jesus from her, she does two things. She shares with the townspeople that the man (Jesus) knows all about her life with the words, "a man who told me everything that I have ever done!" (4:29). Despite their negative attitude toward the woman, these revealing words entice the villagers to follow her to Jesus. Additionally, to ensure that they accept her invitation, the insightful woman adds the rhetorical question, "He cannot be the Messiah, can he?" (4:29). As a result of her invitation, the villagers follow her to the well to meet Jesus.

The villagers accept the woman's invitation, not because they trust her, but out of curiosity about what else Jesus knew about her. The woman's question about his being the Messiah only enhanced his credibility regarding what he could tell them about the woman. Although they followed the woman out of curiosity, her selfless invitation to them altered their lives forever.

64. If women were seen as less intelligent than men, why did Jesus keep using them to spread the word of God, as in the Samaritan woman story? Why, if Jesus related to and respected women, wouldn't the men of those times follow suit?

John 4's inclusion of the unnamed woman at the well in dialogue with Jesus places her in a very important role. Clearly, Jesus does not see her as less intelligent than men. When we contrast her deepening faith in Jesus with the earlier misunderstanding of Nicodemus in John 3 or the later misinterpretation by the disciples of Jesus' conversation with the woman in 4:27, it becomes clear that in these two narratives, true wisdom and insight come from the Samaritan woman, not the men in these scenes. They do not yet seem to grasp either the words of Jesus or that the center of his mission includes both women as well as men.

While one of the purposes of this story is to reveal the conversion of Samaritans into the Johannine communities, another is to affirm the reverent treatment of women by Jesus. However, unlike Jesus' respect for and inclusion of women in his ministry, many men of that time were so predisposed by societal prejudices, that they could not view women objectively. Moreover, it became very difficult for men to even know the thoughts, hopes, and dreams of women because of the strict separation between them imposed by their culture. Unless within the family, in business dealings, or in worship, ancient society in Palestine opposed conversation or contact between men and women. While a mother would somewhat influence her male child, the boy would spend more time with his father and learn about women from him and other male relatives. Since the adult male figure did not have solid knowledge about the topic, prejudices about women passed from one generation to the next. Even though Jesus broke this barrier of discrimination against women, other men did not because of inherited cultural mores.

65. How did Martha know Jesus could raise her brother from the dead in John 11? Why did Jesus let Martha's brother die in the first place?

No textual evidence suggests that Martha knew that Jesus could raise her brother from the dead. In the reading of John 11:1–3, both Martha and her sister Mary tell Jesus that their brother has taken ill, but they request nothing directly. Later, in 11:20–27, Martha welcomes Jesus and has a profound dialogue with him. Nowhere in the text does the Evangelist indicate that Martha knew what Jesus would do to alleviate the situation.

The question, "Why did Jesus let Martha's brother die in the first place?" has a partial response in 11:4, when Jesus says to his disciples, "This illness does not lead to death; rather, it is for God's glory, so that the Son of God may be glorified through it." Surely, the author plays on the words, *death, life,* and *glory* in this story. Like the previous sign in John 9, the healing of the man born blind, the glory of God through Jesus signifies the purpose of both miracles. The Johannine Jesus brings life to others and glorifying him signifies the response of true believers. Furthermore, the gift of a returned life to Lazarus anticipates the gift of eternal life to all who believe in Jesus.

66. In John 11, why is Martha shown as the one who believes in Jesus when in Luke's Gospel it is Mary who is viewed as the one with faith?

When you read both texts carefully, you will notice that neither Luke 10:38–42 or John 11:1–3, 20–27 indicate that Martha's faith in Jesus has been questioned. In both stories, Martha's deep belief in Jesus remains intact. The story of Martha, Mary, and Jesus as a houseguest appears within Luke 10, a chapter that highlights the actions and behavior of true discipleship. As you may recall from the response to Question 42, Martha has been described as a leader, who had concern regarding her service (*diakonian*) to others. This Greek term, *diakonian*, refers to an authorized leader in the community in the early Church. Thus, Martha represents one who ministers, preaches to the community, and supports the members.

In the Lukan story, Martha seeks the help of her sister, who does not come to her aid. In response, Jesus says that, "Mary has chosen the good (*agathen*) part." The Greek term, *agathen*, refers to "good," not better, as in the English translation. In this pronouncement story, Jesus encourages Martha to listen to his word for spiritual nourishment. Never in this narrative does Jesus question her faith in him.

In John 11, Martha welcomes Jesus outside her home at the death of Lazarus, where again she functions as head of the house. Like Luke 10, the themes of discipleship and friendship come in at this mournful time for family and friends. In both stories, Martha models faithful discipleship and leadership. Her fidelity to Jesus comes from her close loving friendship with him.

Her conversation in John 11:20–27 emphasizes the leadership initiative of Martha as she interacts with Jesus. From the outset, Martha speaks freely to Jesus about the death of her brother, an indication of her deep trust in him. Throughout the verbal exchange, Martha's belief in Jesus cannot be shaken. Topics in verses 20–27 range from trust in God to future and present resurrection. As a trusting and close friend, Martha responds openly to Jesus, who finally reveals to Martha, "I am the resurrection and the life. Those who believe in me, even though they die, will live, and everyone who lives and believes in me will never die." This deep self-revelation reminds us of Jesus' open dialogue earlier in John 4 with the woman of Samaria, whom he entrusted with the announcement of messiahship. Here in John 11, however, Martha, rather than Jesus, proclaims, "You are the Messiah, the Son of God, the one coming into the world" (11:27). Martha's threefold christological testimony comes before the raising of her brother Lazarus. It authenticates her profound belief in the person of Jesus, a faith that does not depend on miracles or promises.

67. In John 19:26, is it possible that Mary Magdalene was the Beloved Disciple?

Only the Gospel of John mentions the "beloved disciple" in four places: John 13:23–26; 19:26–27; 20:2–10; 21:20–23. An obvious reason some scholars identify the Beloved Disciple as male comes from the use of the words *son* and *he* in these texts. Traditionally, the Beloved Disciple has been identified as John, son of Zebedee. Recently, however, other possibilities, such as, John Mark or Lazarus, have been suggested. John 19:25, the preceding verse, poses a challenge. Here the Evangelist identifies only the women who stood near the cross while Jesus hung on it to die. His description of only women supporting Jesus correlates with the previous three Gospel accounts.

As a result of this clear indication of women supporters, Sandra Schneiders (*Written That You May Believe*, 203–7) suggests that we need to reconsider the gender and person of the Beloved Disciple. Among the many reflective and scholarly points of her argument, she suggests that the word *son* in the directive, "Woman, here is your son" (19:26), represents the gender of Jesus who speaks, rather than the person to whom he entrusts his mother. In this way, the one who replaces Jesus now relates to the mother of Jesus and protects her like a son would do. Moreover, when Jesus addresses the person, he does *not* say "son," but only "Here is your mother" (19:27). In the same verse, the one to whom Jesus speaks has been named as a "disciple," a term in John's Gospel that includes women. With these and other such arguments, Schneiders concludes that we cannot assume that the "Beloved Disciple" was male. Finally, she posits that if Jesus addressed one of the women who stood near the cross, the likely choice would have been Mary of Magdala.

It is clear that scholarly discussion of the identification of the Beloved Disciple will continue.

68. In John 20:11–18, the empty tomb is first discovered by women. Why is this passage skipped in the readings for the Sunday after Easter?

On Easter morning, the Gospel reading for cycles A, B, and C are from John 20:1–9, the discovery of the empty tomb by Mary of Magdala. On the following Sunday in all three cycles again, the Gospel reading comes from John 20:19–31, the two appearances to the disciples. The story in John 20:11–18 that lies between these two readings is omitted. This important Johannine Gospel story does not appear in any Sunday liturgy, but has been relegated to the Tuesday of Easter week.

Why, then, has John 20:11–18, the risen Jesus' first and only appearance to an individual, namely, Mary of Magdala, been skipped? The answer lies with the liturgical commission that decides the assignment of readings. Given that the Mary of Magdala material in this is one of the most important pieces of information on the prominence of women leaders in the early Church, the decision to omit it from the Sunday readings seems suspicious. Such decisions and the results that follow go against the intention of the Fourth Gospel, which highlights women's leadership in the Christian communities.

As Sandra Schneiders remarks: "If the material on women in the Fourth Gospel were released from the shackles of male-dominated exegesis and placed at the service of the contemporary church, there is little doubt that it would help to liberate both men and women from any remaining doubts that women are called by Jesus to full discipleship and ministry in the Christian community." She adds that God's word in the New Testament "is a word of lib eration intended…for each succeeding generation of believers who will faithfully and creatively address new questions to the text in the well-founded expectation that this Word is indeed living and active" (*Written That You May Believe*, 114). Unfortunately, decisions that exclude the Gospel proclamation of this important directive from the risen Jesus to Mary of Magdala in Sunday liturgical cele-bration further silences this crucial text and deadens the word of God, which is intended for all Christians to hear and celebrate.

69. In John 20:15, why didn't Mary Magdalene realize that it was Jesus and not the gardener who spoke to her?

In John 20, after she discovers the empty tomb, Mary of Magdala's focus is on finding the missing Jesus. She runs back to report her findings and returns to the tomb. With the frustration and worry over the missing body, Mary was overcome with anxiety. In 20:11, 13, the Evangelist describes the state and cause of Mary's grief: "But Mary stood weeping outside the tomb…" because, as she herself says, "they have taken away my Lord, and I do not know where they have laid him."

Anyone who has experienced weeping knows that it represents the deepest form of sorrow. When one weeps, the eyes swell and vision blurs. In this physical and emotional state, it is understandable that Mary did not recognize Jesus standing in front of her. After her unexpected and perplexing discovery of the empty tomb and the appearance of two angels (messengers), she was filled with confusion. Mary would have never expected a visit from a resurrected Jesus. Additionally, Jesus' appearance was different because of his risen state.

In any case, Mary did come to recognize Jesus as he called and addressed her personally with "Mary!" The divine call by name is a strong biblical tradition in the Hebrew Bible, (e.g., Exod 3:4; 1 Sam 3:4), a moment when the divine voice awakens the one chosen. In John 20:16, the same point applies.

As the risen Jesus beckons Mary by name, her recognition of his voice and acknowledgment of call leads her to a new phase in her vocation to follow Jesus. Mary is the first witness of the Easter event, the first to see Jesus in his risen state, and the only one commissioned by him to tell the others what she has experienced. To this woman Jesus entrusts the message that will change the lives of Jesus' followers for all times.

70. In John 20, why did Jesus first reveal himself to Mary Magdalene instead of the apostles at the time of his resurrection? Why, then, isn't Mary Magdalene considered an apostle?

Your question about "picking Mary Magdalene instead of the apostles," needs clarification. The Evangelist of the Fourth Gospel does not refer to Jesus' inner group of followers as "apostles."

Nowhere in the Gospel of John has this term been used. In its place, the word *disciples* describes his close companions.

As I have already mentioned, this Evangelist promotes their importance and leadership among the Johannine communities. Consequently, Jesus' choice of Mary to bring the vital resurrection and ascension message to the others, places her in a position of great importance both within these communities and in the Church in general.

Why, you ask, isn't Mary Magdalene considered an apostle? Fortunately, you have been misinformed. Mary of Magdala has indeed been considered an apostle from early Christian times. Since the Gospel of John does not use the term, *apostle*, I am using it in a technical sense as one who has seen the risen Lord, been commissioned by him, and preaches the good news to others. All these experiences, which have been divinely bestowed on her, result in Mary of Magdala being the first apostle of the risen Lord. By being appointed to tell the other disciples, she becomes a true leader.

Mary of Magdala has been revered since early Christianity as the "apostle to the apostles." As such, she becomes the model and standard of Christian praxis and faith. The term, *apostola apostolorum* ("apostle to the apostles") for Mary of Magdala was used by the early Church as far back as in the preaching and writing of bishop and martyr Hippolytus of Rome in the third century CE. In recent times (1969), the Roman Catholic Church reiterated her importance by officially designating her *apostola apostolorum* ("apostle to the apostles").

Chapter 6

The Acts of the Apostles

71. Why in Acts 1:13–14 is Mary, the mother of Jesus, the only woman identified by name?

The evangelist who wrote the Gospel of Luke also wrote a second volume, called Acts of the Apostles. Except for the infancy narrative (Luke 1 and 2), his portrayal of women in both volumes often minimizes the importance of women leaders in the early Christian Church. This is also true of Acts 1, with the naming of only male apostles and the absence of female names, except for Mary, the mother of Jesus. Gail O'Day proposes that "The anonymity of the remaining women in the upper room suggests that women do not have equal standing with men in this gathering" ("Acts," in *WBC*, 396).

As for the inclusion of Mary, Luke has not spoken of her since the beginning of the third Gospel. By naming only the mother of Jesus in Acts 1:14, Luke links the two books that he has authored into a theological cohesion. Since in Luke 1:38, Mary has remained a true believer and disciple from her initial positive response to the angel about giving birth to Jesus, she now continues her fidelity to God and her son by being a part of giving birth to the Church in Acts 1 and 2. In both instances, the prophetic Spirit of God will overshadow the mother of Jesus as she continues life among Jesus' disciples.

72. In Acts 9:39, what is the significance of the widows "weeping and showing tunics and other clothing" that Tabitha/Dorcas made when alive?

Note that in the beginning of this story (Acts 9:36), Tabitha/Dorcas is identified as a "disciple." As "disciple," Luke classifies her as a leader and a distinguished example of a faithful follower of Jesus. His use of the two names, Tabitha (Aramaic) and Dorcas (Greek), suggests that this respected woman was highly regarded by both groups because she "was devoted to good works and acts of charity" (9:36).

At her death the grieving widows, who had lived and worked with Tabitha/Dorcas, displayed tunics and other clothing that she had created for those in need. This fine clothing reveals the tremendous bond between her and the widows as well as their deep respect and appreciation for her as leader and disciple. Thus, her deep love and selfless service to widows and those in need is emphasized. In essence, Tabitha/Dorcas the "disciple" shines as a role model of selfless giving in time, talent, and money.

73. Given the customs of the period, why is Priscilla named before her husband in Acts 18:26?

The prominent leader, Priscilla, along with her husband, Aquila, have been immortalized predominantly through the writings of Luke and Paul. Paul uses her familial shortened name of Prisca, suggesting a close friendship with her. The names of the couple appear six times in the Acts of the Apostles and in some Pauline and non-Pauline Letters (Acts 18:2, 18, 26; 1 Cor 16:19; Rom 16:3; 2 Tim 4:19). Four of these times, Priscilla's name appears before her husband, an unusual placement in the first century CE. On Bible lists, the first named is usually the most important person.

While they worked together as partners on a team, Priscilla would not have been Aquila's subordinate. Some suggest that the placement of Priscilla's name before her husband's is due to the distinguished social status of her family. Aside from this opinion, Priscilla's prominence emerges from her untiring efforts and leadership within the growing Christian movement. Priscilla ministered in such places as Rome, Corinth, and Ephesus. Her involvement with the continued religious education of the great Apollos in Acts 18 and in saving Paul's life in Ephesus (Rom 16:3) clearly demonstrate her influence and respect given her by others. Consequently, in their writings, both Paul and Luke honor Priscilla in her prominent leadership and missionary accomplishments.

74. In Acts 25 and 26, who is Bernice?

In Acts 25 and 26, Bernice is the great-granddaughter of Herod the Great, the daughter of Herod Agrippa I. Her birth into the royal family in 28 CE conferred power and fame. Her father, who had previously lived many years in Rome, became friends with the Emperor Claudius and thus cemented strong relations between his Jewish family and the Roman aristocracy. However, Luke reports the death of Herod Agrippa I in Acts 12:20–23 and so his position as king went to his son and Bernice's brother, Herod Agrippa II. In these chapters, Bernice and her brother, Herod Agrippa II, arrive in Caesarea Maritima to welcome the new Roman governor, Porcius Festus. This Roman governor succeeds Felix, a Roman governor with whom the Jews were not pleased. In order to ease the tension with the Jews, the new governor, Festus, invited King Agrippa II and his sister/wife, Bernice, to hear the self-defense and plight of a Jewish prisoner named Paul of Tarsus. Acts 25 and 26, then, center on the decisions of the new governor regarding the prisoner named Paul, the arrival of the Jewish royalty in Caesarea, and at the request of King Agrippa, Paul's third recounting of his conversion story to the king and his sister, Bernice.

Chapter 7

Paul's Letter to the Romans

75. In Romans 1:26–27, why is homosexuality referred to as a "degrading passion," a practice that deserves death?

It is important to note that this entire passage in Romans 1 does not highlight homosexuality. Rather, Paul inserts this sexual practice as one of the many actions that he contends go contrary to God. The deeper issue of Romans 1:18–32 centers on the *broken relationship between God and humanity.* According to Paul, when persons reject God, they act in inhuman ways.

This passage in Romans 1:18–32, which includes references to homosexuality, centers on the *clear rejection of God by humans.* This theme recurs repeatedly. In 1:25 the statement, "because they exchanged the truth about God for a lie," speaks of people who have rejected God and the truth that comes from the Divine. According to Paul, then, a break in their relationship with the Divine, leads them to other actions. In first-century CE Judaism, intercourse was mainly for the purpose of procreation in a context of ritual purity. It consisted of one active partner and one passive one. The dominant person penetrated the subordinate one. As you can guess, women would have been considered passive partners.

Therefore, particularly in Judaism, homosexuality makes no sense. For some men to "reduce" themselves to a female role with other men, was considered deeply shameful. At the same time, it would have been inconceivable to have two female passive partners for a homosexual act. Bernadette Brooten mentions that for Paul, women in same-gender relationships defy the order of creation according to Genesis 2, a text that Paul quotes in 1 Corinthians 11:8f, where woman "comes from man" and "for the sake of man" (*Love Between Women: Early Christian Responses to Female Homo-eroticism*, 240). Overall, the offensive element here would have been the blurring of the dominant and subordinate roles of the genders. Ancient Jews thought such actions highly offended God's plan of creation. Again, Romans 1:26–27 must be seen in the context of the entire passage, which focuses on people's rejection of God. Therefore, the topic of homosexuality appears as one of its consequences in Paul's eyes. He places this causal action among other topics such as envy, strife, deceit, craftiness, gossip, etc. Paul's point, therefore, leads to the conclusion that we all dishonor God at times. Thus, he adds in Romans 2:1: "Therefore, you have no excuse, whoever you are, when you judge others; for in passing judgment on another you condemn yourself."

76. Why are so many women named in Romans 16?

The text of Romans 16 offers many examples of women who have been placed in important leadership positions in the early Church. In this chapter, Paul presents himself as a very compassionate and grateful colleague to the women whom he addresses. The verses identify designated Christian women with authentic ecclesiastical roles, such as, those of "deacon" and "apostle." Clearly, Paul greets these women as colleagues, who lead others as he does. Both women and men engaged in all types of ministry to the Christian communities as they worked side by side.

Altogether ten women can be identified in Paul's concluding chapter in Romans, including Phoebe, Prisca, Mary, Junia, Tryphaena, Tryphosa, Persis, the mother of Rufus, Julia, and the sister of Nereus. This extensive list indicates his great respect for these women as well as the hope that their influence will bring him acceptance by the Roman communities, whom he has yet to visit.

77. Why does Paul think that women shouldn't be a voice in the Church, but yet in Romans 16, Phoebe is described as a deacon?

Paul does *not* indicate that women's voices should be silenced in his letters. Paul recognizes and supports fellow women leaders throughout his letters. At times, he even calls them coworkers, as you will notice in Romans 16:3.

The second part of your question about Phoebe being a deacon is very important. The Greek term for deacon (*diakonos*) appears in 16:1 to describe Phoebe's leadership role within the Christian communities. Unfortunately, this technical term has been mistranslated in some versions of the Bible. Some English translations do not honor Phoebe as a deacon, an official title of an office-holder. Instead, they translate *diakonos* as *servant* or *minister*, which suggests a subordinate role.

More specifically, Paul identifies Phoebe as "a deacon of the church at Cenchreae." As "deacon," Phoebe would have functioned as a leader in the liturgical and religious life of the Christians who resided there. More than likely, her home served as a household Church where local communities would gather for the breaking of the bread.

From these two brief verses in Romans 16, Paul honors Phoebe as "deacon," "benefactor," leader, and close friend. His trust in her leadership qualities and her friendship ran so deep that he entrusted Phoebe as the carrier of this important letter to the Romans. Assuredly, he chose Phoebe because of her revered reputation among the Christian churches.

78. Since there were obviously women deacons like Phoebe in the early Church, how and when did that custom change?

Actually, today, women in various Christian churches do have the opportunity to become deacons. In other traditions, however, women's ordination of any kind has been suppressed. Recall that the Apostle Paul also demonstrates a clear partnership with women, who function as leaders in Christian circles. Both in the Pauline letters and in the Acts of the Apostles, women served in important roles as heads of households, deacons, apostles, and disciples. Therefore, women's ministerial roles prove to be very significant in the beginnings of the Church. For example, Paul identifies Phoebe as "deacon" in Romans 16:1. According to many scholars including Ute Elsen, who studied literary and epigraphical inscriptions as well as Church documents, the practice of ordaining women as deacons lasted in both the Greek and Latin Churches throughout the first millennium (*Women Officeholders in Early Christianity*, chapters 5, 7, 8). These women served in cities, villages, and even monasteries.

The office of woman presbyter/presbytera (*presbutera*), a Greek word translated as "priest," exists even today in its masculine form during the ordination ceremony for Roman Catholic and Episcopal priests. From early Christian times and for many centuries thereafter, women held the ecclesial role of "presbyter." Literary documentation about this practice appears in the writing of Bishop Epiphanius, a third-century author, as well as from the documents of the Synod of Laodicea in Asia Minor from the fourth century CE.

Finally, Ute Elsen discusses the role of women bishops. The New Testament offers only a few references to the Greek term, *episkopoi*, translated as "bishop" (Acts 20:28; Phil 1:1; 1 Tim 3:2; and Titus 1:7). In these examples, the term and office of an *episkopoi* is not defined because the term was used so loosely. In later centuries, however, as the Church developed a hierarchical structure similar to the Roman Empire, the term took on a more definite usage referring to leadership. Women leaders designated as bishops appear as late as the ninth century CE in Italy. This is just a glimpse of the history of ordained women in the Church.

79. In Romans 16, Paul addresses Prisca as his "fellow worker in Christ Jesus." Does this mean she was a disciple or a Church leader?

In Romans 16:3, Paul indicates that Prisca served different Christian communities as an equal partner in leadership with Paul. According to Acts 18:1–3, after Prisca and her husband Aquila were expelled from Rome, she served with Paul in Corinth and Ephesus (1 Cor 16:19; Acts 18:26).

As a leading minister, Prisca would have hosted weekly liturgies in her house, supplied hospitality to itinerant preachers like Paul, and led the local Christian communities in numerous ways. In particular, the fact that Paul places Prisca's name before her husband's in Romans 16:3 demonstrates her importance as a vital leader respected by the communities of Rome. Since she had previously lived there, she would have known and befriended members of the Christian communities in different parts of the city. Consequently, their familiarity with Prisca and her husband allows Paul to offer high personal praises about them as his close friends.

In 16:4, Paul even goes so far as to remind the Romans of the couple's great courage as he proclaims "they risked their necks for me." This comment suggests the extent to which Prisca and Aquila would go to serve the needs of another, in this case, their close friend Paul. Clearly, in 16:3–4, Paul honors Prisca and shows his gratitude to her for all that she has been to him.

80. In Romans 16:7, Paul calls Andronicus and Junia prominent apostles. Is it possible women (such as Junia) were included in that group? Why were Andronicus and Junia in prison with Paul?

In his writings, Paul never limits the term "apostle" to the Twelve. Furthermore, he is insistent always that he himself exemplifies a true apostle of Christ (1 Cor 1:1; 9:1–2; 15:9–10; Rom

1:1) because he has seen the risen Lord and been commissioned by him to minister to others. These two actions describe an apostle.

Here in Romans 16:7, a woman relative of Paul named "Junia" is also called an "apostle." This verse represents the only text in the entire New Testament that actually uses the word "apostle" to refer to a woman, making Romans 16:7 a very important text indeed. Since this verse has been proclaimed rarely by Christians within the churches, many are not familiar with it and do not realize its significance in the discussion of women leaders within the early Christian communities.

The second half of the verse in Romans 16:7 indicates that Junia, a relative of Paul, functioned in a special way as an apostle, a very honored position within the Christian communities. Paul notes that Junia was also "prominent" among the apostles. This added description identifies her as a woman leader, who was well respected throughout the communities. John Chrysostom, an early Church father and doctor of the Church testifies to this wording. As he comments on Romans 16:7, he declares "It is certainly a great thing to be an apostle: but to be outstanding among the apostles—think what praise that is! She [Junia] was outstanding in her works, her good deeds: oh, and how great is the philosophy of this woman, that she was regarded as worthy to be counted among the apostles!" (*Epist. Ad Rom. Homil.* 31, 2).

Paul's clear identification of Junia as an apostle contradicts the idea that only male apostles existed in the apostolic period. While some have attempted to masculinize Junia's name throughout the centuries, the truth about her identity remains. Paul clearly demonstrates that women were represented and respected on all levels of ecclesial leadership within the Church—including that of apostle.

As for your second question, "Why were Andronicus and Junia in prison with Paul?" no answer can be given. Unfortunately, Romans 16:7 is the only time that Junia and Andronicus are named in the letters of Paul. No other texts exist within the Pauline letters that provide an answer to your question.

Chapter 8

Paul's Letters to the Corinthians, Galatians, Philippians, and Philemon

81. Why in 1 Corinthians 7:1 does it state, "It is well for a man not to touch a woman"? How else could the world continue?

A recent consensus of Pauline scholars concludes that this statement does not come from the thoughts of Paul. Rather, it is a quote from the correspondence that the Corinthians had sent previously to Paul. Here Paul uses their quote to answer them. In 1 Corinthians 7, Paul seems disinterested in the married state because he anticipates the second coming of Christ in the near future. For Paul, it is better not to have children if the end is near. He wants the Corinthians to free themselves from any anxieties so as to prepare for the end-times.

How did the Corinthians view marriage? Most likely men living in the Greco-Roman society of Corinth did not view marriage in terms of equality. Rather, they probably agreed with what Demosthenes, a famous Athenian orator, had written years before: "courtesans were companionship, concubines to meet every day sexual needs and wives to tend the house and bear legitimate children" (*Against Neara* 59.122 quoted in Catherine Clark Kroeger, "1 Corinthians," in *IVP Women's Bible Commentary*, 653). Against such a philosophy, Paul honors the practice of having only one wife or husband (7:2) with no other sexual relationships, which goes directly against the tradition of Demosthenes. Instead, Paul addresses the marriage state in this passage in terms of respect and equality in sexual matters (7:4). Ultimately, his directives in 1 Corinthians 7 do not prohibit intercourse between married couples, but encourages thoughtful decisions about the act in the belief that the end-time would come soon.

In all correspondence, it is important to realize that directives, such as this one in 1 Corinthians 7, were addressed to a specific community with particular issues. Such letters were never intended to be used universally. They remain situation specific.

82. 1 Corinthians 11:3 says, "and the husband is the head of his wife." What was the author trying to say?

Keep in mind that, as a whole, 1 Corinthians 11 centers on proper dress and behavior during liturgical functions. Consequently, all questions concerning issues within this chapter need to be answered within this context. In addition, scholars have found this chapter very difficult to interpret over the years because of the obscurity of Paul's words.

When Paul says "the husband is the head (*kephale*) of his wife," he uses a formula to place a sense of order in the universe and creation. The Greek term, *kephale*, translated here as "head," also means "origin" or "source." The latter translation becomes more important in this verse. In Genesis 2, the earlier Creation story, the woman comes from the man. As such, he represents her "source," rather than her "head." Therefore, in 11:3, when Paul mentions "Christ," "husband," "wife," he speaks about relationships. Furthermore, these associations in divine and human categories suggest the need for interdependence.

83. In 1 Corinthians 11:2–16, what do hairstyles and head coverings signify? Why is this an issue? In verse 6, what is the significance of women

shaving off their hair if they won't veil themselves? Is the veil similar to the *hijab* worn by Muslim women?

As mentioned above, the entire argument surfaces as the first part of a threefold discussion of proper behavior and dress within the context of liturgical worship. Hairstyles and hair coverings have often represented the stance, social position, and religious practices of a person, as demonstrated in 11:2–16. Interestingly, nowhere does Paul use the term, *veil*, but a broader Greek term, *kalypto*, translated as "head covering."

Some scholars view the discussion within the cultural framework of honor and shame, where Paul urged women prophets to cover their heads so as not to shame themselves and shock others. In Corinthian society, women with uncovered or shaven heads may have been slaves or prostitutes. Paul replaces the astounding statement about cutting off a woman's hair with the more moderate act of head covering (11:6) in an effort to recognize that these Corinthian women without head coverings were respected leaders within their Christian communities rather than shameful outcasts.

Your question, "Is the veil similar to a *hijab* worn by Muslim women for purposes of modesty?" demonstrates a fine observation. Women in ancient times and in many cultures today cover their heads for the sake of modesty. This act of religious significance originates from early cultural norms. The ancients believed that a woman's hair reflected her beauty. Therefore, only her husband should see it. They also held that women with uncovered hair distracted and even tempted men. This position has remained in some religious practices and cultures even to the twenty-first century.

84. In 1 Corinthians 11:7, Paul says man is a reflection of God and woman is a reflection of man. Why does he say this if God created us all in his own image? Why isn't more made of Genesis 1:27—"So God created humankind in

his image, in the image of God he created them; male and female he created them"—regarding women in the modern Church?

Your question relates to the Creation story found in Genesis 1:1—2:4a, written hundreds of years after the earlier Creation story in Genesis 2:4a–25. When Paul explains the relationship between woman and man, he reflects back on the earlier Creation myth in Genesis 2, where the man becomes the "source" for the woman. In this discussion, he does not refer to the second Creation myth in Genesis 1 about the equality of woman and man.

When Paul uses this comparison in 11:7, he says that man "is the image and glory of God." Yet, when Paul speaks of "woman," he calls her only a "reflection of man." In typical rabbinic argumentation on Genesis 2, he proves his point with a play on words and their associations with each other. While Paul never denies that woman represents the "image of God," he doesn't affirm it either. Instead, he refers to the Creation story in Genesis 2, which focuses on the bond between the woman and the man. Their lives were meant to be relational.

Remember that these remarks in 11:7 are made within the argument on head coverings. Even though the sense of the verse seems obscure, Paul's reasoning centers on the issue of head coverings within liturgical worship and roles of women and men within these assemblies. While seeming to abandon true logic in his argument, he reverts to the traditions of honor and shame. A woman's head needs to be covered in worship, while a man's head does not. This point reflects the accepted traditions in worship at that time.

85. It appears that 1 Corinthians 11:11–12 contradicts the sentiment of the rest of chapter 11. Why?

1 Corinthians 11:11–12 continues the argument about head coverings within liturgical worship. Paul does not contradict his statements in reference to the first Creation myth in Genesis 2;

rather, he nuances them. In light of the previous remarks that gave a strong leaning to the strength of man, Paul tries to affirm the mutuality between the genders by reminding them that they both need each other and God. One of his most important statements in these verses comes with his remark that for both woman and man "all things come from God" (11:12).

In these two verses, then, Paul affirms mutuality, reverence, and the need of God for both genders. Subsequently, both have the divine call and opportunity to serve in leadership positions of prayer, prophecy, and liturgical assembly. Since Paul's remarks appear within the argument for head coverings, however, both women and men still need to observe proper dress in worship, dress acceptable to society. Such remarks from Paul appear in the verses that follow 11:11–12.

86. In 1 Corinthians 14:34–36, why is it shameful for a woman to speak in church when in Romans 16:1 there is a female deacon?

Your question about 14:33–34 represents a very valid inquiry because these verses ruin the flow of the argument within the entire passage. As you notice in your biblical text, these verses are set off in parentheses. This suggests that they appear questionable in their context and might not come from the original author.

The most plausible explanation seems to be that 14:34–36 does indeed represent an interpolation, a later insertion made by an editor and not by Paul. Otherwise, the regulation that "women should be silent in the churches" because "they are not permitted to speak, but should be subordinate...," makes no sense considering Paul's other views about the leadership of women in the liturgy. Ultimately, then, these verses should not be included in Paul's discussion of women's leadership because they do not represent the thoughts of Paul himself.

Whoever the author might be, it seems that he aims to pull back on Paul's promotion of women as liturgical leaders. By redacting Paul's original intention, the unknown author gives more credibility to the withdrawal of authority from women leaders in the churches. Inserting this into the authentic letter of Paul paves the way for the restrictions on women leaders in the pastoral letters.

87. In 1 Corinthians 16:19 and 2 Timothy 4:19, Paul writes that the Church met in Priscilla's house. Was she the hostess of the home, the leader of the house Church, or both?

Since Paul writes the Letter to the Corinthians from Ephesus in Asia Minor, he would have been with Prisca (Priscilla) and Aquila, who had moved there from Corinth. The implication in 16:19 would be that Paul sends greetings from the church that meets in their home. As for 2 Timothy 4:19, Paul did not write this letter, but a later author also mentions Prisca and Aquila, a sign of their continued leadership within the household Churches.

Recall that Prisca served as a leader within the Christian communities. She was renowned for her role as teacher and leader of household Churches in all the references about her in both the Pauline letters and Acts of the Apostles. Moreover, Paul's comments surely indicate that their home would have hosted the local church both in liturgy and hospitality for itinerant preachers like himself. Prisca and Aquila would have provided Paul with food, shelter, safety, and patronage so that he could work in Ephesus and travel to his next mission (Mary Ann Getty-Sullivan, *Women in the New Testament*, 161). Furthermore, they would have worked together in their mutual trade of tent making (Acts 18:3), which means more broadly, workers in the leather trade, for needed funding to carry out their other works.

Additionally, the house of Prisca and Aquila would also be a place of learning for new converts. The married couple would have taught these groups. Clearly, Paul and Prisca worked as coworkers in the mission at Ephesus.

88. In Galatians 3:28, Paul says, "There is no longer Jew or Greek, there is no longer slave or free, there is no longer male and female; for all of you are one in Christ Jesus." Doesn't this prove all are equal through Jesus Christ? Why doesn't the rest of the New Testament have the same philosophy?

The powerful text of Galatians 3:28 reiterates what it means to be incorporated into the Church community, where after being baptized "there is no longer Jew or Greek, there is no longer slave or free, there is no longer male and female; for all of you are one in Christ Jesus" (3:28). Now, truly we become one through Jesus Christ because previous religious background, gender, and social status cease to matter when we enter the Christian community. This radical and transformative statement acts as guide in faith as well as liturgical practice.

The principle, "neither male nor female" mirrors Genesis 1:27, where both male and female are created equal under God. In this way, Galatians 3:28 reflects a new creation, that of a new community under Christ. Members of this community are not limited by differences because they participate in unity with one another.

However, Galatians 3:28 has not always been recognized as an emancipation proclamation for women. While unity in Christian community may be recognized, equality between the genders is challenged. Many modern scholars quote it as a freedom piece in Christ, while others see it as promise for a much distant future. This latter stance translates into women being relegated to a lower status than men ecclesiastically.

To answer your question about, "the rest of the New Testament philosophy," remember that the New Testament represents the thoughts, ideas, and concerns of many authors, time frames, and situations, not one. This being said, we know that each individual author has a unique view of Christ, God, and community. Subsequently, their ideas about the status of women will also differ.

89. In Philippians 4:2, why does Paul want to help these two women who have fought?

In Philippians 4:2–3, it becomes clear that a problem arose between two women leaders, who probably ministered under the guidance of Lydia. While Paul never mentions the issue at hand, he does write about his concern for these women and its effect on the church in Philippi. Quarrels of any type between ecclesial leaders often damage the morale of the churches that they serve. While disagreements will occur among leadership, charity must be the final outcome for the good of all. Clearly the dispute between the two women has caused uneasiness among the members of the community.

In 4:2, Paul "urges/appeals" to them twice: "I appeal (*parakalo*) to Euodia and I appeal (*parakalo*) to Syntyche to be of the same mind (i.e., to come to mutual understanding [*phronein*] in the Lord)" (my translation). His double appeal indicates that these two women held important positions in the church at Philippi. Since Paul's prime message in this entire letter centered on unity, this friction needed to be eliminated so that these two women leaders could be healed and tend to their responsibilities. To make a greater impact for healing, Paul urges "mutual understanding" (*phronein*). The Greek term, *phronein*, in 4:2, which translates literally to "set one's mind," has the connotation of agreement or a meeting of the minds. The women must agree, must have a meeting of the minds, so that they again may be one in union with Christ, their center. By modeling Christ, they can continue to unify both themselves and others in their leadership and labors.

90. In Philippians 4:3, what is the "book of life" that contains the names of women and men?

In Philippians 4:3, the "book of life" can refer to one of two things: Hellenistic cities that registered their citizens, or the "book of life" in the Israelite tradition. In the Hebrew Bible, righteous people will be in God's good graces and written in the "book of life." God chooses people to be in the "book of life" even before they exist (Psalm 139:16). On the other hand, according to Exodus 32:31–33 and Psalm 69:28, sinners will be blotted out of the book. Here in Philippians 4:3, when Paul refers to names written in the "book of life" in reference to Euodia and Syntyche, he demonstrates his great respect and trust in their leadership qualities. At the same time, Paul exhibits his esteem for them as persons and friends as he declares that "they have struggled beside me in the work of the gospel." Therefore, he calls them "co-workers," a title that identifies them as quite close to Paul in the mission at Philippi.

91. In Philemon 1:2, Apphia is referred to as "our sister." Does this mean a sister in Christ or an actual relative?

At the beginning of the letter, Paul includes the name of "Apphia" in the formal greeting because of her importance within the community. Apphia was a common Phrygian name found on several ancient inscriptions in that area. The phrase, "Apphia our sister" in verse 2 signifies a very close relationship with Paul. Some commentators maintain that she may be the wife of Philemon; others disagree. No one suggests that she and Paul were related by blood. In the letter to Philemon, the reference to "our sister" indicates that she has been a coworker with Paul in the mission of the early Church.

Pheme Perkins suggests that Apphia could have been a patron of the community ("Philemon," *WBC*, 453). In this capacity, she would have led the community in many ways and had influence over the members. Possibly, Apphia played a leadership role in the Christian communities even before Paul came to evangelize. Whatever the case, she seemed to be on equal terms of leadership with Paul in these early days of Christianity. In the address of the letter, Paul incorporates the name of Apphia so that she, too, will try to reason with Philemon about his runaway slave, Onesimus, in the hopes that Philemon, his master, will forgive him.

Chapter 9

Other Letters and the Book of Revelation

92. Why does Ephesians 5:22–23 say that wives are to be subject to their husbands who are the head of the house? How does that fit with our modern sense of equality?

Ephesians 5:22–23 does not fit with views on equality in marriage for people in developed countries today. Rather, these post-Pauline thoughts appear within a household code (5:21—6:9) that focuses on relationships in a married household. It expands the same topics found in Colossians 3:18—4:1. Unlike Paul, who promoted women in decision-making roles, these Deutero-Pauline authors do not.

The instruction, "wives, be subject to your husbands" in 5:22, as well as in Colossians 3:18, matches the mores of the Greco-Roman times. The ancients considered households a working microcosm of the whole society. Households had a paterfamilias (father of the family), and the husband ruled with absolute power over his family members and servants. Greco-Roman society believed that God/the gods intended this so that harmony would continue in this pyramidal ruling structure of both society and household.

In Ephesians, the anonymous author softened the custom of absolute power of the husband with the preceding directive in 5:21, which presents a theological justification for submission of the wives, "Be subject to one another out of reverence for Christ."

While this statement lessens the absolute power of the husband over the wife, it still fosters the husband's superior relationship to her. The wife remains under the authority of her husband with all the degrading subjection of being his property.

Unlike Paul, who promoted women, this author attempts to make Christianity acceptable to Roman society. Amidst persecution and rejection, some leaders and writers like this author tried to conform more to cultural traditions regarding women, so as not to be seen as an enemy of the state. Subsequently, the idea of women as leaders within the Christian communities or as mutual partners in marriage must be sacrificed. Such texts, like the household code, reflect these attempts.

93. It says in Ephesians 5:33 that women are to respect their husbands and husbands are to love their wives. Why is differentiation made between respect and love? Wouldn't you think those two ideas/feelings need to be given and received by both wife and husband in a successful marriage?

Some of the directives in the household code, such as 5:33, make us uncomfortable with the Western world's contemporary mode of thought about marriage. As I have already suggested in the previous response, in order to understand and appreciate the thoughts of this anonymous author about marital relationships, the historical context must be understood. Clearly, the Church in the latter part of the first century CE and early second century CE experienced rejection and persecution from Roman society, who viewed them as an enemy. The freedom that women and slaves had within Christian communities went against the accepted traditions of the larger society. Therefore, this point represents one of the many reasons why Rome viewed Christianity with great suspicion.

Once again, the statement in 5:33 that the husband "should love his wife as himself, and a wife should respect (*phobetai*) her husband," reflects an attempt to mirror somewhat the larger society. While modern translators often use the less offensive translation of *respect*, the Greek term, *phobetai*, literally means "fear." The expectation of a wife was that she would be totally subject to the authority of her husband, like all other members of the household including children, other household members, and slaves.

Subsequently, the author urges love from the husband toward his wife, but for the wife, he urges obedience and respect. Unlike our modern-day thoughts on marriage, where we expect both "love" and "respect" between marriage partners, in 5:33, the married partners do not share equality, but the wife lives under the control and authority of her husband.

94. In 1 Timothy 2:12, who is the "I" who will "permit no woman to teach or have authority over a man"?

The "I" in 1 Timothy 2:12 seems to be an anonymous pastor and/or the author of the letter. This verse appears within a set of household codes (2:8–15), namely, the household of God which signifies the Church. Amidst other concerns about worship within the communities, 2:12 appears within a number of directives to the behavior of women during worship service. The prohibition reflects the mores of the Greco-Roman society, where women could teach male children, but not male adults.

As for not having "authority over a man," the anonymous author bases this statement on the Genesis 2 Creation story, where God created the woman after Adam. Furthermore, this author has a faulty memory of Genesis 3, the Garden scene, when he proclaims "Adam was not deceived but the woman was deceived and became the transgressor." A quick reading of Genesis 3 clearly disproves this view, because Adam was also deceived and ate the forbidden fruit.

This incorrect interpretation of Genesis 3, which became the excuse for forbidding women leadership, has no basis. Such negative injunctions have caused terrible repercussions upon women throughout the centuries and history of the Church, all due to a faulty interpretation of Genesis 2 and 3, and conclusions that the original biblical texts in Genesis never intended.

95. In 1 Timothy 2:15, why does the "I" in verse 12 think women "will be saved through childbearing"?

The concept of women being saved through childbearing relates to previous verses in 2:13–14 that declare Eve "a transgressor" because she ate the forbidden fruit and went against the divine command (Gen 3:6). In 2:15, the author/pastor declares that women, despite transgressions, can come again into God's graces in the capacity of a mother. In the tradition of first-century society, the author/pastor promotes "childbearing" as a way to promote faith and to add to the number of future Christians in the communities.

According to this author, salvation differs for men and women, which is not the case in other books of the New Testament. By separating the paths of salvation between the genders, the author severs any equality between them as fellow Christians. As a result, men have the upper hand, even within worshipping communities. Benjamin Fiore, SJ, comments "after characterizing women as inherently subordinate…as insignificant and unreliable, removed from a public role in the church, the author of the letter had to assure women of a place of significance and holiness. This place for them was the home in the fulfillment of socially expected domestic duties" (*The Pastoral Epistles: First Timothy, Second Timothy, Titus*, 69). Thus, statements like those found in 1 Timothy 2:15 promote the domestication of women in the private place and implicitly oppose the authority of women in the public sphere.

96. In 1 Timothy 5:9, what type of list were widowed women put on if they became widows after the age of sixty and had only married once? Why no lists for men in the same categories? For what was the list used?

The directive about widows after the age of sixty being put on a "list" emerges amidst an entire section about this group (5:3–16) according to circumstances and age. Plainly, these women were a concern for the local churches because of their financial needs and pressing circumstances. Both in the Hebrew Bible and New Testament, stories about widows and their hardships abound.

Since this entire section about widows in 1 Timothy 5 has been placed under the broader instructions regarding leadership (4:12—6:2), some qualify for special categories, such as the "real widow," who needed to be at least sixty years old, left alone without family support, and praying night and day (5:5, 9). Widows would be put on "the list" for communal financial support after they met the criteria established in these directives. It also seems likely that the widows on "the list" had an official role within the community. In this letter, the author appears to have little or no concern for younger widows who needed financial assistance. They appear only as a problem. In 5:6, he condemns a widow "who lives for pleasure," meaning she works as a prostitute to meet the financial needs for herself and her children. If the younger widow has no other family members to provide for her or her offspring, the author/pastor does not offer assistance. Once again, a widow remained totally dependent on the mercy of others.

Widowers did not need to be put on any list. Unlike widows, they could work publically and receive financial payment. Therefore, they did not need organized charity from the community.

97. In 1 Timothy 5:15, why are young widowed women sometimes considered followers of Satan?

In 1 Timothy 5:11–15 the definition of *widow* narrows and applies to young widows with whom the author finds fault. Unfortunately, he unfairly attributes the bad behavior of a few to the entire group and condemns all the women who fall into this category. In verse 15, he criticizes the behavior of some young widows by declaring that they "have turned away to follow Satan."

Moreover, such negative portrayals of the young widows suggest that the author did not trust them to teach others. Consequently, through such biting criticism, the author attempts to narrow the office of widows, namely to those women eligible for the list (1 Tim 5:9). He directs that the general category of all widows be limited to older destitute women who would cause no scandal for the churches.

98. In Titus 2:3–5, why are self-control, goodness, and submissiveness of women connected to the word of God being either credited or discredited?

The detailed directives regarding women in the letter of Titus appear within the broader regulations of the household code for the communities of Crete. The prohibitions as well as positive instructions in 2:3 pertain specifically to older married women, who have been told to be reverent and to teach goodness. The list of proper behaviors for them continues in the next two verses with instructions to encourage young women to love their husbands and children, to be "self-controlled, chaste, good managers of household" and above all to be "submissive to their husbands" (2:4–5). Following all this advice would make them model Roman wives within the larger society.

The last part of 2:5, namely, "so that the word of God may not be discredited," is the only part of the entire instruction that includes a specifically Christian directive. The list of Roman virtues sacrifices freedom and a fuller life for Christian wives in order to achieve respectability within society. The author attempts to promote obedience and submissiveness to their husbands in order to have these mature women conform to the role of the Roman matron in her family. In this way, Christianity will become more creditable to Greco-Roman society.

In essence, conformity to the conditions set forth by the author does not necessarily credit or discredit the word of God for the woman. In this scenario, the discrediting pertains to the Church being accepted by the Greco-Roman society. If Christian wives act like Roman wives, their behavior will be positive in the eyes of the larger community. Thus, the word of God will be credible in the public eye.

99. In 1 Peter 3:1–6, wives are taught to "accept the authority" of their husbands. Is that correct?

Yes, in these verses, wives are taught to accept the authority of their husbands, an instruction that emerges from household codes in 1 Peter 2:18—3:7. The author commands wives to center their lives on "purity and reverence" rather than external extravagances such as gold jewelry and clothing. He also calls for obedience toward their non-Christian husbands and promotes submissiveness toward them for the sake of conformity with the practices of both Greco-Roman society and Judaism. According to the author's belief, obedience in these other areas will give strength to the wives to stand firm in their faith and not be forced to practice the religion of their husbands. When the author says "never let fears alarm you" (3:6), he addresses this very point to the wives trying to remain firm in their own faith.

Today many societies realize that such unfortunate advice has led to abuse and victimization of wives. Now, rather than encourage passive and blind obedience of one human being to another, Western society supports mutual respect and equality in a marriage. Only when a wife is viewed as a true partner with her husband, will love, honor, and respect prevail.

100. In Revelation 12:1–2, who is this pregnant woman with "a crown of twelve stars"?

Contrary to popular notions, the crowned pregnant woman does *not* represent Mary, the mother of Jesus. The imagery is much broader and inclusive. This fascinating symbol of a pregnant woman with twelve stars as a crown symbolizes fullness in the people of God. The "crown of twelve stars" represents Israel with the twelve tribes, which gave birth to Christianity.

Later in 12:2, the author sates that the woman "was crying out in birth pangs." This imagery evokes memories of Genesis 3:15 where God speaks to the serpent in the Garden after Adam and Eve ate the forbidden fruit. He says "I will put enmity between you and the woman and between your offspring and hers." In the following verse (Gen 3:16), God addresses the woman about pain in childbearing with the words, "I will greatly increase your pangs in childbearing; in pain you shall bring forth children."

Thus, the woman in the sky represents victory over all suffering and iniquity. This age-old symbol of conflict has been resolved. Good triumphs over evil. As you can envision, all these collective symbols are fluid in the interpretation of this passage, but signify common themes of good versus evil represented by various mythical figures in many religions throughout the ancient world.

101. In Revelation 14:4, the text warns against men defiling themselves with women. Why would anyone consider a male/female relationship as defilement?

An initial reading of Revelation 14:4 is potentially disturbing to any reader, especially a woman, because it suggests that women make men unholy through intercourse. However, we need to remember that the Book of Revelation, like other biblical texts, often contains multilayered meanings and must not be taken literally. Revelation 14:4 is such a case.

According to the Hebrew Bible, soldiers were not to have any sexual relations with their wives when they served in a holy war (Exod 19:15; 1 Sam 21:4–6). At these times, the men believed that they fought alongside God, and, therefore, needed to refrain from any distractions to keep their bodies pure for the Divine. In this case, then, the imagery evokes a battlefield.

Another interpretation of verse 4 refers to abstention from sexual intercourse with young virgins chosen for service in the liturgical rites of pagan temples. Since many early Christians came not only from Judaism, but also from polytheistic religions in the Greco-Roman Empire, this sacred rite of intercourse would have been familiar and possibly even practiced by them before entering Christianity. In this case, the author warns men against former practices.

Whatever the intended meaning, this verse does not have to do with intercourse between married couples. The author never intended that interpretation. Moreover, throughout the Book of Revelation, sexual meanings often refer to spiritual infidelity toward the Divine. Therefore, this verse could also be interpreted in this way. But it cannot be interpreted to make women the source of men's temptation and failure, as often it has been in the past.

Select Bibliography

Anderson, Janice Capel. "Matthew: Gender and Reading." *Semeia* 28 (January 1983): 3–26.

Banks, Robert. *Paul's Idea of Community.* Peabody, MA: Hendrickson Publishers, Inc., 1994.

Bassler, Jouette. "1 Corinthians." In *Women's Bible Commentary.* Expanded Edition. Edited by Carol Newsom and Sharon Ringe, 411–19. Louisville, KY: Westminster John Knox Press, 1998.

Baumert, Norbert. *Woman and Man in Paul.* Collegeville, MN: The Liturgical Press, 1996.

Blessing, Kamila A. "John." In *IVP Women's Bible Commentary*, edited by Catherine Clark Kroeger and Mary J. Evans, 584–605. Downers Grove, IL: IVP, 2002.

Boyarin, Daniel. "Paul and the Genealogy of Gender." In *A Feminist Companion to Paul*, edited by Amy-Jill Levine, 3–18. Cleveland: The Pilgrim Press, 2004.

Brock, Ann Graham. *Mary Magdalene, the First Apostle, the Struggle for Authority.* Cambridge, MA: Harvard University Press, 2003.

Brooten, Bernadette. "Junia...Outstanding among the Apostles." In *Women Priests: A Catholic Commentary on the Vatican Declaration*, edited by Leonard and Arlene Swidler, 141–44. Mahwah, NJ: Paulist Press, 1977.

————. *Love Between Women: Early Christian Responses to Female Homoeroticism.* Chicago: University of Chicago Press, 1996.

Brown, Raymond. *The Gospel According to John.* Two Volumes. The Anchor Bible Series. Garden City, NY: Doubleday, 1966.

Brown, Raymond, Karl P. Donfried, Joseph Fitzmyer, and John Reumann, eds. *Mary in the New Testament.* Mahwah, NJ: Paulist Press, 1978.

Byrne, Brendan, SJ. *Romans.* Sacra Pagina Series. No. 6. Collegeville, MN: The Liturgical Press, 1996.

Cardman, Francine. "Women, Ministry and Church Order in Early Christianity." In *Women & Christian Origins,* edited by Ross Shepard Kraemar and Mary Rose D'Angelo, 100–29. New York: Oxford University Press, 1999.

Carter, Warren. "Getting Martha out of the Kitchen: Luke 10:38–42 Again." *Catholic Biblical Quarterly* 58:2 (April 1996): 264–80.

Castelli, Elizabeth. "Romans." In *Searching the Scriptures,* edited by Elisabeth Schüssler Fiorenza, 272–300. New York: Crossroad, 1994.

Chittister, Joan. *WomenStrength.* New York: Sheed and Ward, 1990.

Chrysostom, John. *Epist. Ad Rom. Homil.* 31, 2.

Clement of Alexandria. *Stromateis.* Books 1–3. Translated by John Ferguson. Washington, DC: Catholic University of America Press, 1991.

Cohick, Lynn. *Women in the World of the Earliest Christians.* Grand Rapids, MI: Baker Academic, 2009.

————. "Romans." In *The IVP Women's Bible Commentary*, edited by Catherine Clark Kroeger and Mary J. Evans 628–45. Downers Grove, IL: InterVarsity Press, 2002.

Collins, John N. *Diakonia: Re-Interpreting the Ancient Sources.* New York: Oxford University Press, 1990.

Collins, Raymond. *First Corinthians.* Sacra Pagina Series. Collegeville, MN: The Liturgical Press, 1999.

Conzelmann, Hans. *1 Corinthians.* Hermeneia Bible Commentary Series. Edited by George MacRae, SJ. Philadelphia: Fortress Press, 1975.

Corley, Kathleen. *Women & and the Historical Jesus.* Santa Rosa, CA: Polebridge Press, 2002.

Cousar, Charles B. *The Letters of Paul.* Nashville, TN: Abingdon Press, 1996.

D'Angelo, Mary Rose. "Mark 14:3 9." In *Women in Scripture*, edited by Carol Meyers, 434–36. New York: Houghton Mifflin Co., 2000.

————. "Martha." In *Women in Scripture*, 114–20. edited by Carol Meyers New York: Houghton Mifflin Co., 2000.

De Boer, Esther A. *The Gospel of Mary: Listening to the Beloved Disciple.* New York: T & T Clark International, 2004.

Dewey, Joanna. "1 Timothy." In *Women's Bible Commentary.* Expanded Edition. Edited by Carol Newsom and Sharon Ringe, 444–49. Louisville, KY: Westminster John Knox Press, 1998.

Donahue, John, and Daniel Harrington. *The Gospel of Mark.* Sacra Pagina Series. Edited by Daniel Harrington. Collegeville, MN: Liturgical Press, 2002.

Dowsett, Rosemary. "Acts of the Apostles." In *The IVP Women's Bible Commentary*, edited by Catherine Clark Droeger and Mary J. Evans, 606–27. Downers Grove, IL: InterVarsity Press, 2002.

Drury, Clair. "The Pastoral Epistles." In *The Oxford Bible Commentary*, edited by John Barton and John Muddiman, 1220–33. Oxford, UK: Oxford University Press, 2001.

Elliott, Karen, C.PP.S. *Women in Ministry in the Writings of Paul.* Winona, MN: Anselm Academic, 2010.

Elsen, Ute. *Women Officeholders in Early Christianity: Epigraphical and Literary Studies.* Collegeville, MN: Liturgical Press, 2000.

Epp, Eldon Jay. *Junia: The First Woman Apostle.* Minneapolis, MN: Fortress Press, 2005.

Fiore, Benjamin, SJ. *The Pastoral Epistles: First Timothy, Second Timothy, Titus.* Sacra Pagina Series. Edited by Daniel Harrington. Collegeville, MN: The Liturgical Press, 2007.

Fiorenza, Elisabeth Schüssler. *In Memory of Her.* New York: Crossroads, 1990.

———, ed. *Searching the Scriptures: A Feminist Commentary.* 2 Vols. New York: Crossroad Publishing, 1994.

Gaventa, Beverly Roberts. *Mary: Glimpses of the Mother of Jesus.* Minneapolis, MN: Fortress Press. 1995.

———. "The Gospel of Mary." In *The Complete Gospels*, edited by Robert Miller, 257–366. San Francisco: Harper, 1994.

Gench, Frances Taylor. *Back to the Well: Women's Encounters with Jesus in the Gospels.* Louisville, KY: Westminster John Knox Press, 2004.

Getty-Sullivan, Mary Ann. *Women in the New Testament.* Collegeville, MN: Liturgical Press, 2001.

Gillman, Florence. *Women Who Knew Paul.* Collegeville, MN: Liturgical Press, 1992.

Gregory the Great. *Homiliarum in evangelia,* Lib. 11, *Patrolgia Latina,* vol. 76. Paris: J.-P. Migne, 1844–1864, cols 1238–1246.

Green, Joel. *The Gospel of Luke.* Grand Rapids: William B. Eerdmans Publishing Co., 1997.

Hays, Richard. "Paul on the Relation between Men and Women." In *A Feminist Companion to Paul,* edited by Amy-Jill Levine, 37–54. Cleveland: The Pilgrim Press, 2004.

Hock, Ronald. *Infancy Gospels of James and Thomas.* Santa Rosa, CA: Poleridge Press, 1995.

Ilan, Tal. *Jewish Women in Greco-Roman Palestine.* Peabody, MA: Hendrickson, 1996.

Jensen, Anne. *God's Self-Confident Daughters, Early Christianity and the Liberation of Women.* Translated by O. C. Dean, Jr. Louisville, KY: Westminster John Knox Press, 1992.

Johnson, Elizabeth. "Ephesians." In *Women's Bible Commentary.* Expanded Edition. Edited by Carol A. Newsom and Sharon H. Ringe, 428–32. Louisville, KY: Westminster John Knox Press, 1998.

Johnson, Luke T. *The Gospel of Luke.* Sacra Pagina Series. Edited by Daniel Harrington. Collegeville, MN: Liturgical Press, 1991.

Josephus, Flavius. *Against Apion; The Jewish War; Jewish Antiquities.* Loeb Classic Library. Translated by Henry St. John Thackeray. Cambridge, MA: Harvard University Press, 1981.

Keener, Craig. *Paul, Women and Wives: Marriage and Women's Ministry in the Letters of Paul.* Peabody, MA: Hendrickson Publishers Inc., 1992.

Kieffer, Rene. "John." In *The Oxford Bible Commentary*, edited by John Barton and John Muddiman, 960–1000. Oxford, UK: Oxford University Press, 2001.

Kraemer, Ross Shepard. *Her Share of the Blessings: Women's Religions among Pagans, Jews, and Christians in the Greco-Roman World.* Oxford, UK: Oxford University Press, 1992.

Kraemer, Ross Shepard, and Mary Rose D'Angelo. *Women & Christian Origins.* New York: Oxford University Press, 1999.

Kroeger, Catherine Clark. "1 Corinthians." In *The IVP Women's Bible Commentary*, edited by Catherine Clark Kroeger and Mary J. Evans, 646–64. Downers Grove, IL: InterVarsity Press, 2002.

Kung, Hans. *Women in Christianity.* Translated by John Bowden. London: Continuum, 2001.

Longstaff, Thomas, R.W. "What Are Those Women Doing at the Tomb of Jesus: Perspectives on Matthew 28:1." In *A Feminist Companion to Matthew*, edited by Amy-Jill Levine and Marianne Blickenstaff, 196–204. Sheffield, UK: Sheffield Academic Press, Ltd., 2001.

MacDonald, Margaret. "Virgins, Widows, and Wives: The Women of 1 Corinthians 7." In *A Feminist Companion to Paul*, edited by Amy-Jill Levine, 154–69. Cleveland: The Pilgrim Press, 2004.

Malina, Bruce. *The New Testament World: Insights from Cultural Anthropology.* Louisville, KY: Westminster John Knox Press, 2001.

Martyn, J. Louis. *Galatians.* The Anchor Bible Series. Edited by William Foxwell Albright and David Noel Freedman. New York: Doubleday, 1997.

————. *The Mishnah.* Translated by Herbert Danby. London: Oxford University Press. 1972.

Miller, Robert, ed. *The Complete Gospels.* San Francisco: Harper Collins, 1994.

Moloney, Francis. *The Gospel of John.* Sacra Pagina Series no. 4. Edited by Daniel Harrington. Collegeville, MN; The Liturgical Press, 1998.

Murray, Robert, SJ. "Philippians." In *The Oxford Bible Commentary*, edited by John Barton and John Muddiman, 1179–90. Oxford, UK: Oxford University Press, 2001.

Myers, Carol, ed. *Women in Scripture.* New York: Houghton Mifflin Co., 2000.

Newsom, Carol, and Sharon Ringe, eds. *Women's Bible Commentary.* Expanded Edition. Louisville, KY: Westminster John Knox Press, 1998.

Newsom, Carol, Sharon Ringe, and Jacqueline Lapsley, eds. *Women's Bible Commentary.* Twentieth-Anniversary Edition. Louisville, KY: Westminster John Knox Press, 2012.

O'Day, Gail R. "Acts." In *Women's Bible Commentary.* Expanded Edition. Edited by Carol A. Newsom and Sharon H. Ringe, 394–402. Louisville, KY: Westminster John Knox Press, 1998.

————. "John." In *Women's Bible Commentary Expanded Edition.* Edited by Carol A. Newsom and Sharon H. Ringe, 381–93. Louisville, KY: Westminster John Knox Press, 1998.

Osiek, Carolyn. "Galatians." In *Women's Bible Commentary*. Expanded Edition. Edited by Carol A. Newsom and Sharon H. Ringe, 423–27. Louisville, KY: Westminster John Knox Press, 1998.

———. "The Women at the Tomb: What Are They Doing There?" In *A Feminist Companion to Matthew*, edited by Amy-Jill Levine and Marianne Blickenstaff, 205–20. Sheffield, UK: Sheffield Academic Press, Ltd., 2001.

Pagels, Elaine. *The Gnostic Gospels*. New York: Random House, 1979.

Perkins, Pheme. "Philippians." In *Women's Bible Commentary*. Expanded Edition. Edited by Carol Newsom and Sharon Ringe, 433–36. Louisville, KY: Westminster John Knox Press, 1998.

———. "Philemon." In *Women's Bible Commentary*. Expanded Edition. Edited by Carol Newsom and Sharon Ringe, 453–54. Louisville, KY: Westminster John Knox Press, 1998.

Reid, Barbara. *Choosing the Better Part? Women in the Gospel of Luke*. Collegeville, MN: The Liturgical Press, 1996.

Reimer, Ivoni Richter. *Women in the Acts of the Apostles*. Translated by Linda Maloney. Minneapolis: Fortress Press, 1995.

Ringe, Sharon. H. *Luke*. Louisville, KY: Westminster John Knox Press, 1995.

Ruether, Rosemary Radford. *Women-Church*. San Francisco: Harper & Row, 1985.

———. *Women of Spirit*. Eugene, OR: Wipf and Stock Publishers, 1998.

Sabin, Marie Noonan. *The Gospel According to Mark.* Collegeville Bible Commentary Series. Collegeville, MN: Liturgical Press, 2006.

Sakenfeld, Katharine Doob, ed. *The New Interpreters Dictionary of the Bible.* Nashville: Abingdon Press, 2009.

Sampley, Paul. *Paul in the Greco-Roman World, A Handbook.* Harrisburg, PA: Trinity Press International, 2003.

Schaberg, Jane. "Luke." In *Women's Bible Commentary.* Expanded Edition. Edited by Carol Newsom and Sharon Ringe, 363–80. Louisville, KY: Westminster John Knox Press, 1998.

Schneiders, Sandra. *The Revelatory Text.* Collegeville, MN: Liturgical Press, 1999.

————. *Written That You May Believe.* New York: Crossroad Book Company, 2003.

Schubert, Judith. *The Gospel of John: Question by Question.* Mahwah, NJ: Paulist Press, 2008.

Stanton, G. N. "Galatians." In *The Oxford Bible Commentary,* edited by John Barton and John Muddiman, 1153–65. Oxford, UK: Oxford University Press, 2001.

Swan, Laura. *The Forgotten Desert Mother: Sayings, Lives and Stories of Early Christian Women.* Mahwah, NJ: Paulist Press, 2001.

Tannehill, Robert. C. *Luke.* Nashville: Abingdon Press, 1996.

Thurston, Bonnie, and Judith Ryan. *Philippians & Philemon.* Sacra Pagina Series. Edited by Daniel Harrington. Collegeville, MN: Liturgical Press, 2005.

————. *Women in the New Testament.* New York: Crossroad Publishing Co., 1998.

Tolbert, Mary Ann. "Mark." In *Women's Bible Commentary*. Expanded Edition. Edited by Carol Newsom and Sharon Ringe, 35–62. Louisville, KY: Westminster John Knox Press, 1998.

Torjesen, Karen Jo. *When Women Were Priests*. San Francisco: Harper Collins Publishers, 1993.

Twelftree, Graham. "Demon." In *The New Interpreter's Dictionary of the Bible*. Vol 2. Edited by Katharine Dobb Sakenfeld, 91–100. Nashville: Abingdon Press, 2007.

Wagner, Lilya. "Galatians." In *The IVP Women's Bible Commentary*, edited by Catherine Clark Kroeger and Mary J. Evans, 680–94. Downers Grove, IL: InterVarsity Press, 2002.

Wainwright, Elaine. *Shall We Look for Another? A Feminist Rereading of the Matthean Jesus*. Maryknoll, NY: Orbis Books, 1998.

Weren, Wim. "The Five Women in Matthew's Genealogy." *Catholic Biblical Quarterly* 59:2 (April 1997): 288–305.

Williams, Ritva. *Steward, Prophets, Keepers of the Word: Leadership in the Early Church*. Peabody, MA: Hendrickson Publishers, 2006.

Wils, Gray. *What Paul Meant*. New York: Viking Penguin, 2006.

Winter, Bruce. *Roman Wives, Roman Widows*. Grand Rapids, MI: William B. Eerdmans Publishing Co., 2003.

Wire, Antoinette Clark. *The Corinthian Women Prophets: a Reconstruction through Paul's Rhetoric*. Minneapolis, MN: Fortress Press, 1990.

Witherington, Ben. *Paul's Letter to the Romans.* Grand Rapids, MI: William B. Eerdmans Publishing Co., 2004.

Yamaguchi, Satoko. *Mary and Martha, Women in the World of Jesus.* Maryknoll, NY: Orbis Books, 2002.